the art of collage

More than just a compilation of photos, journaling, and memorabilia, scrapbooking is an adventure in personal expression. In this selection, exciting techniques let you explore a whole new set of creative possibilities. Find ways to translate your own style through collages using rubber stamps, paper clay, hand tinting, or image transfers. Then stretch these ideas—and your talents—by making an altered book.

make your mark

Rubber stamps, embossing powders, and specialty inks can add a custom touch to your layouts and paper designs.

by Lori Bergmann

Visiting my local scrapbooking store is great fun, but it wasn't always guiltfree. When I first started scrapping, the store also was a large stamping supplier. To reach the scrapping supplies, I had to race through rows of stamps, inks, and powders, telling myself, "Be strong! With four years of albums to catch up on, you don't have time for cards!" Well, times change and the stamping industry now provides products scrapbookers can use with confidence!

Simple Stamping

If you're totally new to rubber stamping, you're probably overwhelmed by the sheer number of stamping products on the market. Luckily, you really need only a few of them to get started.

A stamp. Available in a variety of designs, stamps let you imprint images onto surfaces such as paper, polyshrink, and metal. They come in both unmounted and mounted versions. An unmounted stamp consists just of the foam or rubber design; a mounted stamp includes a wooden or acrylic base that serves as a handle and aids in achieving even application.

An inkpad. Inkpads come with three types of ink—pigment, embossing, and dye-based. Pigment inks are more lightfast than dye-based inks and take longer to dry, making them perfect for embossing techniques. It's best to heat-set these inks to make them permanent and to prevent smudging, and you'll need to emboss them if you're using them on glossy paper.

Embossing inks are similar to pigment inks in that they have a longer open time (the time available to add embossing powder before the ink dries), and they come in only two varieties: clear and lightly tinted.

Dye-based inks are quick-drying and don't need to be heat-set or embossed, but they may fade over time. No matter which type of ink you choose, make sure your selection is acid-free and archival.

A heat-setting tool. Heat-setting tools blow hot air onto ink to permanently set it. They also work well for melting

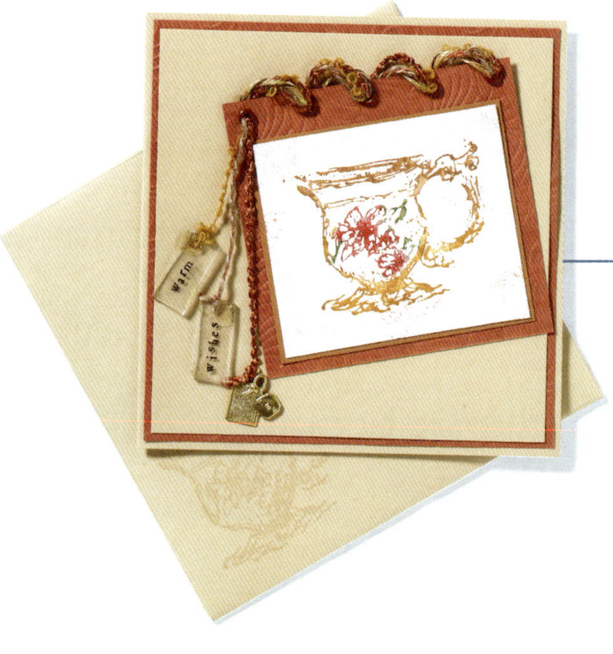

★ Jennifer Ditz used markers to color specific sections of the teacup image before stamping it onto paper. To keep the ink from drying before she had a chance to do the stamping, she huffed on the image, keeping it moist.

Sources: Handmade paper by The Jennifer Collection. Gold Galaxy Marker by American Crafts. Teacup stamp by Art Impressions. Letter stamps by Hero Arts. Fibers by Rubba Dub Dub. Charm by Fancifuls Inc. Shrink plastic by Polyshrink. Envelope template downloaded off Twopeasinabucket.com. Design by Jennifer Ditz.

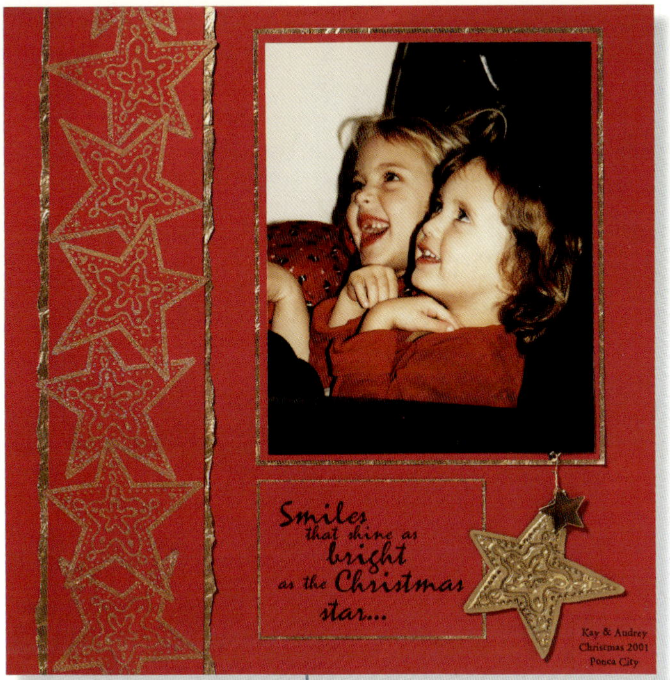

★ The multistar image on this layout was created using a technique called masking. Masking involves covering portions of the surface you'll be stamping so that one image will appear to be in front of another. Designer Jennifer Ditz used Post-it notes to block out areas she didn't want to stamp and heat-embossed the final image. The star accent was made by pressing the stamp into several layers of ultra thick embossing powder.

Sources: Computer fonts are Garamouche (date) by P22 and Aeolus (quote) downloaded off the Internet. Embossing powder by PSX. Ultra thick embossing enamel by Suze Weinberg. Rubber stamp by Great Impressions. Charm by Fancifuls Inc. Design by Jennifer Ditz.

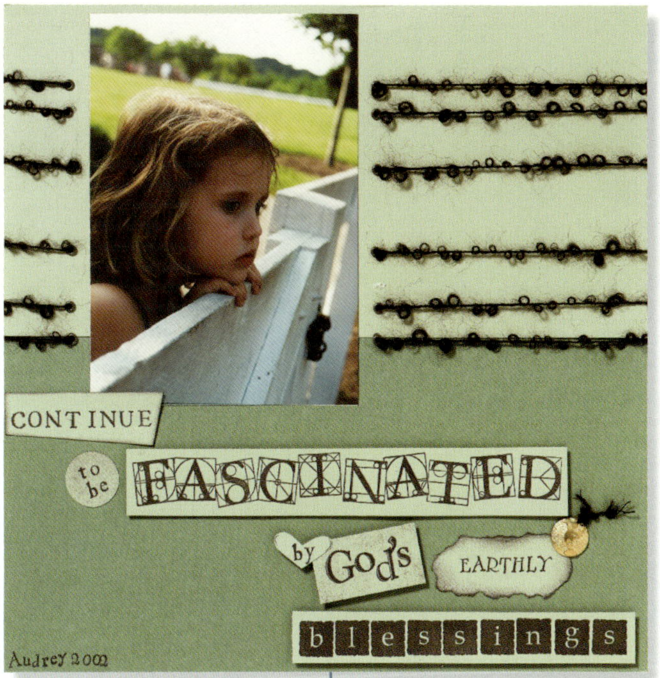

★ Jennifer Ditz selected several different sets of alphabet stamps for the title on this page. She used the masking technique to achieve the overlapping effect on "fascinated." Then to keep the letters in some words straight, she used a temporary adhesive to attach a pencil to the paper as a guide to rest the stamps against.

Sources: Stamps by Hero Arts ("continue to be," "by," "earthly," and "blessings"), Hampton Arts ("fascinated"), and PSX ("God's"). Fibers by Rubba Dub Dub. Charm by Fancifuls Inc. Design by Jennifer Ditz.

embossing powder and polyshrink. Although they resemble hair dryers, the two are not interchangeable. Hair dryers don't reach the temperatures necessary to melt embossing powders, and they blow too forcefully to be used to set inks.

A stamp cleaner. You can use any number of products to clean rubber stamps, such as water-moistened paper towels or washcloths, baby wipes (non-alcohol-based), and commercially sold stamp cleaners. When you need to clean a stamp with a lot of intricate detail, a soft toothbrush comes in handy, too.

Once you've gathered the right supplies, you're ready to begin stamping. Press the stamp onto the inkpad, covering all areas of the image with ink. Then place it on your surface and press down firmly, making sure not to rock or twist the stamp. *Note:* For tips on positioning letter stamps, layering images, or adding multiple colors to images, see Jennifer Ditz's layouts, *opposite* and *above*.

Basic Backgrounds

You can use inks alone or in combination with stamps to create unique background designs that are a nice substitute for patterned papers. Create a randomly spaced design or stamp images closely together to create a seamless pattern that covers the entire page. Try adding a coordinating image as a border, frame, or journal-box accent.

One convenient tool for stamping large backgrounds is a brayer. Brayers resemble small paint rollers and are used to apply wide swaths of color from an ink pad. You also can use a brayer to create patterned backgrounds by painting your design directly on the roller with a water-based pen or paint or by using a textured roller. Fiskars makes a wide brayer with interchangeable rollers in numerous patterns.

ClearSnap also makes a number of tools that work well for background stamping. MagicStamps are moldable foam sheets and shapes that can be heated and impressed with textures from any surface. You can reheat the foam and impress it with new designs again and again for unlimited

make your mark

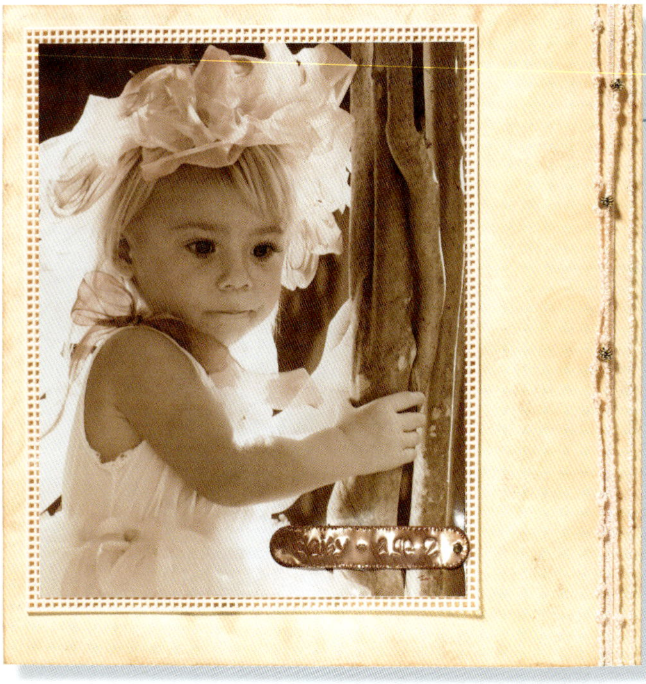

★ To make the blended background for this layout, Erin Terrell rubbed ink pads directly on a sheet of paper. She used a light pigment ink and a dye ink to build up the base color. Then she lightly pressed a metallic ink pad over the entire page for sparkle.

Sources: Inks by ColorBox (brown), Hero Arts (rose), and Tsukineko (copper). Copper tag by InTAGlios. Fibers by Magic Scraps (pink) and Adornaments (pastel pink). Design by Erin Terrell.

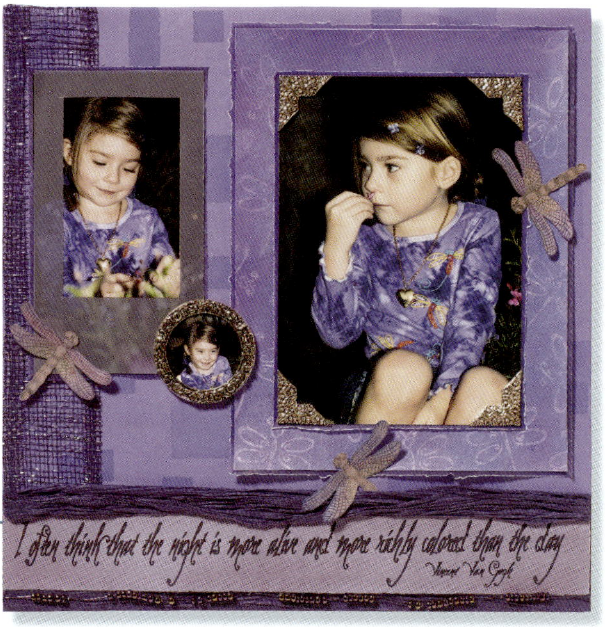

★ For the large mat, use Versamark ink to stamp dragonflies on white paper, then rub purple and blue Radiant Pearls over the paper. Radiant Pearls won't adhere to the Versamark images, creating a subtle pattern.

Sources: Versamark ink pad by Tsukineko. Stamps by Provo Craft (dragonflies) and Hero Arts (square shadow). Purple mesh by Magic Scraps. Metallic beads by JewelCraft. Silver photo corners and frame by Boutique Trims. Design by Erin Terrell.

design possibilities. The company's ColorToolBox product works in a similar manner and comes with moldable foam tips and textures in a range of themes.

Foam stamps also are a great way to design custom backgrounds for your scrapbook pages or accent cards. Inexpensive foam stamps are available in a variety of styles. Rubber Stampede has several new designs, including some geometric patterns that look great on contemporary pages. The stamps are durable and easy to grasp; they range in size from approximately 1 inch to more than 8 inches square.

There also are several ways to add color to your pages without using stamps, such as the direct-to-paper (DTP) technique, in which you transfer color from your ink pad to your paper using the pad as a sort of paintbrush. Shaped removable pads like ClearSnap's Petal Points are among the easiest to use. You also can use texture brushes or sponge applicators to transfer color from bulkier pads or bottles of liquid ink.

Heat Embossing

Heat embossing is a great way to add dimension and texture to a design. The basic technique involves stamping an image with pigment or embossing ink, coating the stamped image with embossing powder, and then heating it until the powder liquifies and the image appears smooth.

Embossing inks come in clear or tinted pads and in pen form for drawing your own designs. You also can emboss directly on some adhesives such as double-stick Magic Tape from Magic Scraps and Zig 2Way Glue from EK Success. Embossing powders come in a range of colors, finishes, and textures. Clear embossing powder is a great staple to keep on hand because it lets you brighten and intensify any ink color underneath it, much like the effect of a coat of polyurethane over stained wood.

When you're ready to try heat embossing, start by preparing your surface. Rub an antistatic pad over the paper before doing any stamping to keep the powder from sticking to areas you don't want embossed.

After stamping, pour a generous amount of powder over the image and tap off the excess. (Pour the excess powder back into the container so you can reuse it.) Hold the heat-setting tool 3 to 4 inches above the coated surface and slowly move it back and forth until you see the powder begin

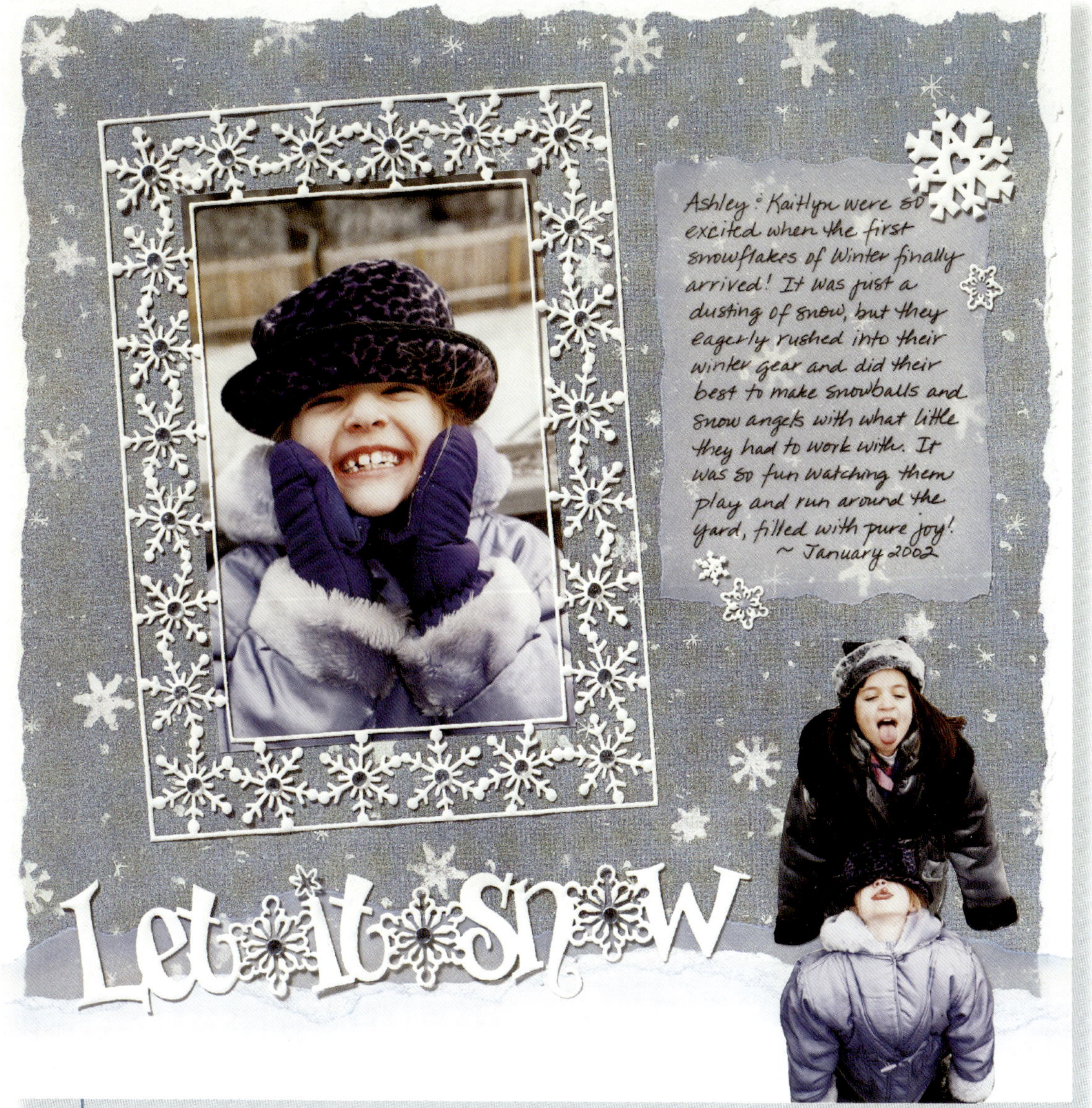

★ Lori used a bottle of embossing ink and a foam applicator to cover the laser-cut frame, title, and snowflake accents with ink before sprinkling with white ultra thick embossing enamel. The rhinestones were stuck in the embossing powder while it was still hot, eliminating the need for gluing.

Sources: Patterned paper and laser-cut frame, title, and snowflakes by Provo Craft. Rhinestones by JewelCraft. White ultra thick embossing enamel by Suze Weinberg. Design by Lori Bergmann.

to melt and change appearance. (This process can take from 5 to 10 seconds or longer, depending on the thickness and type of embossing powder.)

Continue moving the heat-setting tool over the remaining unmelted areas until the entire surface has been embossed, taking care not to overheat the paper or finished areas, which could ruin your project. You can continue to add layers of powder while it's still warm to achieve the effect you want. Be careful not to touch an embossed surface until it has cooled because the powder can be extremely hot—the thicker the layers, the longer they'll take to cool.

You also can get the texture of heat embossing without the heat by using an embossing paste. This thick white or clear medium can be spread directly onto a layout or used with stencils to

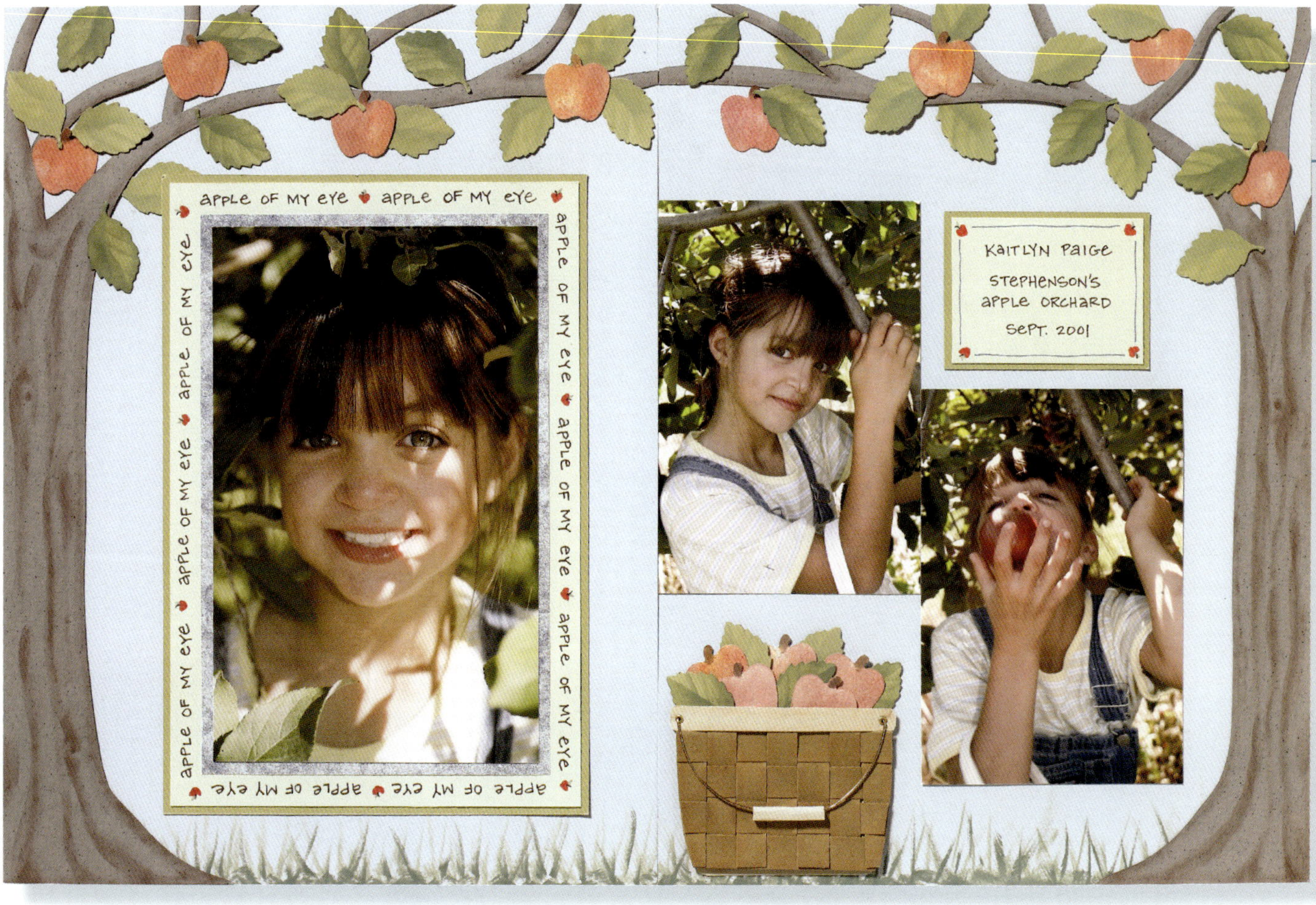

create raised patterns and designs. It's very lightweight, and you also can add glitter or other embellishments to the paste while it's still wet to customize the look. It takes anywhere from 20 minutes to several hours for the paste to dry, depending on how thickly it's applied.

Unique Ink Effects

Stamping inks come in a dizzying array of colors as well as finishes such as matte, pearlescent, and metallic. They can be splattered, sponged, or smeared on paper; dribbled onto acetate for a mottled effect; or painted directly onto stamps. Water-based inks also can be mixed to make custom colors or diluted to produce pastel tones. Here's the lowdown on a few of the more interesting types of ink currently available.

Fresco inks by Stampa Rosa have a soft, chalklike finish and come in beautiful old-world colors, making them ideal for use on vellum, for combining with decorating chalks, and for shadow stamping. Fresco inks have to be heat-set in order to keep them from smudging or fading.

Silk iridescent inks come in brilliant colors and have a luminous sheen that resembles fine silk fabric, making them especially good for large color washes and detail painting. Metallic inks are valued for their rich, lustrous appearance and now come in a much wider range of colors than the standard gold and silver. They can be embossed, applied with DTP (direct to paper) techniques, and used to create elegant accents or bold focal-point designs.

The Nature Print Kit by Ranger uses inks that have a thick, creamy consistency, making them easy to apply to all kinds of natural, dimensional objects.

Pearlescent paints come in several varieties, have a subtle radiance, and are especially useful for creating dreamy background effects or highlights. You also could add a touch of pigment powder (such as Perfect Pearls by Ranger) to plain or Versamark inks for a similar effect.

★ Lori used Fresco inks to give the accents on this layout soft shading, drawing lines and blending colors with a foam applicator. She also wove a basket of brown card stock and attached a wire handle with minieyelets and handwrote the text around the main photo.

Sources: Patterned papers by Provo Craft. Fresco ink pads by Stampa Rosa. ColorToolBox stylus and leaf-shaped foam tip by ClearSnap. Punches by Marvy Uchida (apple) and McGill (birch leaf). Gold minieyelets by Creative Impressions. Design by Lori Bergmann.

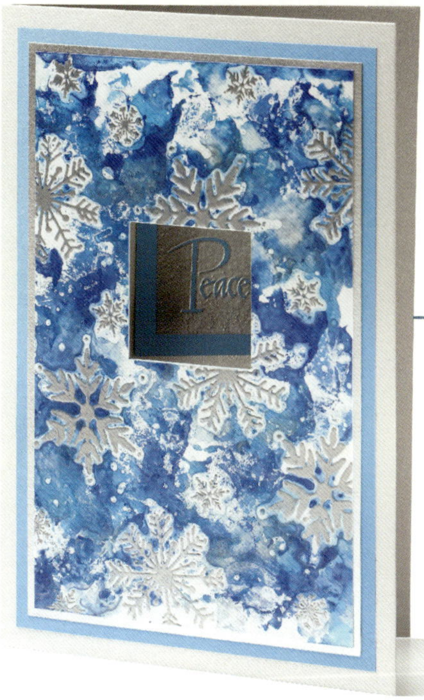

★ Lori created this card by first stamping and embossing several sizes of silver snowflakes on white glossy card stock. She scattered drops of three different colored inks onto a page protector, folded the plastic in half, and used a brayer to spread the colors. Lori then opened the folded plastic, placed the embossed card stock facedown in the inks, and pressed until she had the look she wanted.

Sources: Silver metallic paper by Canford. Blank silver greeting card by Gartner Studios. Silk inks, embossing powder, and rubber stamps by Stampa Rosa. Big & Bossy embossing ink pad, white glossy paper, and rainbow roller brayer by Ranger Industries. Design by Lori Bergmann.

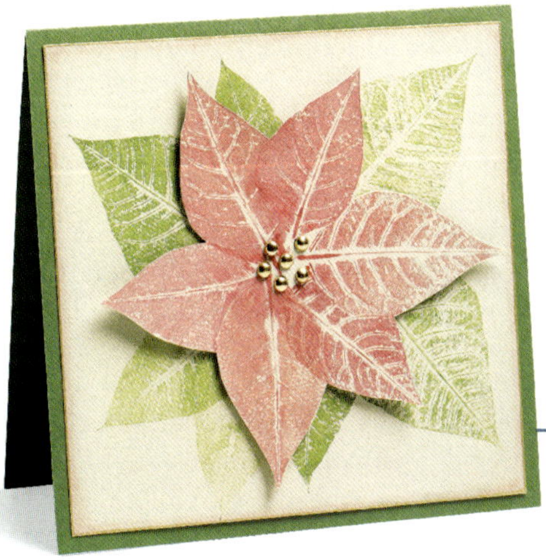

★ Lori sponged Nature Print inks onto several real poinsettia leaves which she then used to stamp on card stock for this lifelike card. She layered the images until she had the shape she wanted and then cut out the flower and attached it to the stamped background with gold brads.

Sources: Nature Print Kit by Ranger Industries. Gold brads by Impress Rubber Stamps. Design by Lori Bergmann.

Most powders will need to be sealed with a fixative to prevent smudging, except Perfect Pearls, which have a built-in fixative.

So, have I tempted you to try some of these ideas and relieved you of the guilt you've felt over coveting stamping supplies? I hope so, because I'm confident that adding even one of these techniques to your scrapbooking toolbox will bring a fresh touch to your pages.

You might even use one to create a card or some other small project once in a while! The key is to experiment and just have fun. And who knows? This could be the start of a new creative passion. |||||

TIPS

When inking a large stamp or when using several colors of ink, huff on the entire image just before stamping to reactivate the ink for best results. Huffing is similar to breathing on your eyeglasses to get them misty before wiping them clean.

Wrap aluminum foil around a large cardboard square and then place it under your design while embossing it to help heat the paper from underneath and cut down on warping.

Unless you're working with a transparent acrylic-mount stamp, assessing where the inked image will end up can be difficult. Thankfully, several tools are available to help you. My favorite is the 2-in-1 Stamp Positioner from Stampa Rosa. It has a large stable base and grid pattern on the bottom for perfect positioning. If you don't have one of these tools, try stamping in a slightly staggered manner for a fun and casual effect or making your own positioner from household objects.

light as a feather

Keep the weight off by using paper clay to make sculpted embellishments and title treatments for your paper projects.

by Sara Tumpane

When I was a child, I spent hours rolling and shaping clay into just about anything imaginable—food, houses, funny faces, and something I believed was my dog Sugar. I loved using my mom's potato masher to make waffle patterns in it, watching the clay ooze through the openings. So when I began scrapbooking, it was only natural for me to add embellishments of clay to the pages!

Paper-Clay Sculpting

Making and adding great clay embellishments to your pages doesn't have to be a weighty process—not if you use paper clay, a great product made of paper pulp that dries so lightweight you may never find an end to its scrapbooking uses!

Best of all, its 8.3 pH rating makes it completely safe to use. And you don't have to be a sculptor to make great-looking designs. If you ever played with clay as a child or rolled out dough to make cookies, you're already well on your way to being a paper clay expert. You can use it to make free-form shapes, rolled strips, stamped designs, beads, graphic elements, charms, template letters, and cookie-cutter shapes. So look at the examples that follow and see just how easy making paper clay accents can be!

Tool Time

Several paper-pulp or papier-mâché clay products are available. The Creative Paperclay Company offers an extensive line of products, including Paperclay and Delight. Both are air-dry products, and while both are quite lightweight, Delight borders on weightless. The Fila Company offers DAS Pronto, a product similar to Paperclay in its consistency, color, and ability to air-dry.

There also are several specially made tools to help you roll and cut as you work with paper clay. A clay roller and clay blade (made by American Art Clay Company and available at arts and crafts stores) are musts, although you can make some low-cost substitutions. A 6-to-8-inch length of 1-inch-thick wood dowel works well as a roller, and a 1×12-inch strip of thick stencil plastic can serve as a blade.

If you want to try more detailed clay accents, pick up a Clay Gun by Lowe-Cornell. It comes with a selection of discs with precut shapes such as circles, squares, and wavy lines. The clay is forced through the cutouts, creating long shaped strands. Another helpful tool is sandpaper. A medium-to-fine-grain sandpaper is the perfect way to remove rough or uneven edges. By rolling up a small piece you can work the sandpaper into small crevices, giving your creation a smooth surface for painting or other decoration.

Plastic gloves will help keep your hands clean. I also recommend covering your work space with plastic or waxed paper before you begin any clay project to prevent mess and ease your cleanup. A sheet of Plexiglas or thick plastic also works well as a smooth work surface.

Getting Started

The best way to familiarize yourself with paper clay is to start simple. Roll out your clay to the desired thickness and cut some geometric shapes such as squares and rectangles. Or press a cookie cutter into the clay just as you would if you were making cookies. Smooth rough spots by dipping your finger in water and rubbing it over the edges. Try pressing a rubber stamp (inked or not) into your rolled clay and cutting out your stamped image with a knife or scissors. Remember, if you don't

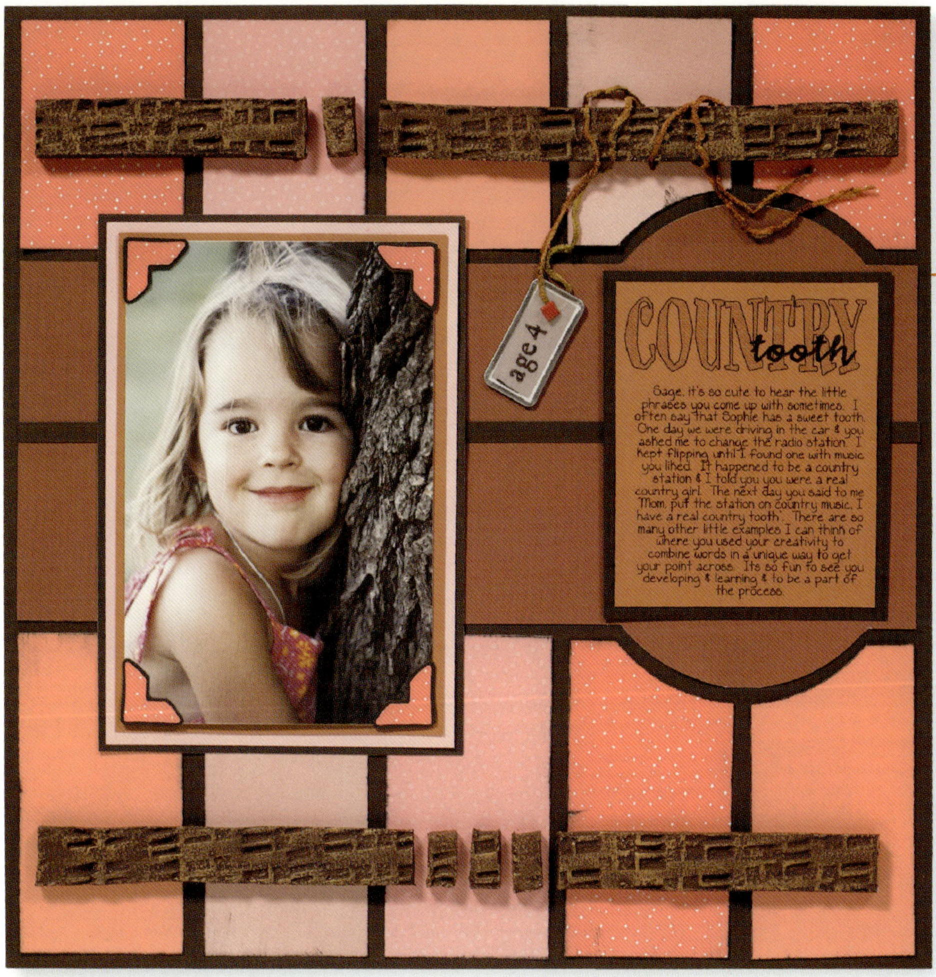

★ Vivian Smith found the chunky texture used to create the pieces on this layout in her daughter's closet! She pushed the sole of one of Sage's hiking boots into the wet clay, lifting the pattern of the tread. She cut the thick, highly textured pieces into strips of different lengths, using them to frame the page, and painted them with acrylic crafts paint.

Sources: Patterned papers by O'Scrap! (pink dots) and Provo Craft (dark pink). Computer fonts are PC Bedrock ("country"), "Fontmania" CD by Provo Craft Hugware, PC Jenn Penn (journaling), and Emma Script ("tooth") downloaded off the Internet. Alphabet rubber stamp by PSX. Photo corner die cuts by Sizzix. Square brad by Provo Craft. Vellum metal-rim tag by Making Memories. Fibers by Rubba Dub Dub. Design by Vivian Smith.

like how something turns out, you can work the clay back into a ball and start over. (If the clay gets dry, knead in a few drops of water.) Allow your designs to dry thoroughly—generally overnight, depending on thickness. You may want to turn over your items in the middle of the drying process to avoid warping or damp spots.

Once dry, you can finish your design in a number of ways. You can treat paper clay items just as you would a sheet of card stock. You can decorate them with chalks, paints, inks, stamps, metallic rub-ons, crystal lacquer, and stickers, and even heat-emboss them! If you want to add texture to your item it's easier to do while the clay is damp. Similarly, if you want to embed something in the paper clay—beads, buttons, or wire—it's best to press them into the clay while damp, then remove them to allow the clay to dry. Once the piece is dry, glue the embellishments into the impressions you've made.

If you can't wait for your accent to air-dry, bake it in your kitchen oven at 250° F for 15 minutes or until dry. *Note:* Delight clay should not be dried in an oven or microwave. Cleanup is easy, too: Paper clay residue washes off your hands and tools with water. Be sure to store unused paper clay in an airtight bag for future use.

Adding Texture

Perhaps one of the best aspects of scrapbooking with paper clay is that it allows you to add texture to your pages. A simple stroll through and around your home will net you many items to create texture in your clay. Virtually anything from a woven basket to tree bark, a metal screen to a roll of wire, a sea sponge to the sidewalk is fair game. Keep your eyes open for anything with a unique texture.

Freshly rolled-out clay is soft, and this is when you should create any texture in the surface. Whether you're creating an all-over texture or stamping a design into your clay, the key is to work it into the clay before it starts drying. Even air exposure during the kneading and rolling process will reduce the moisture level in the clay.

When pressing something into clay, start with light pressure and then increase it for a deeper impression. If you're using something like Magic Mesh to create your texture, you may need to use a scissors tip or stylus to press it deeper into the clay to create a visible texture (pressing with your fingers might be counterproductive). If you find that you've pressed too hard and the clay becomes too thin, simply reroll the clay and try again.

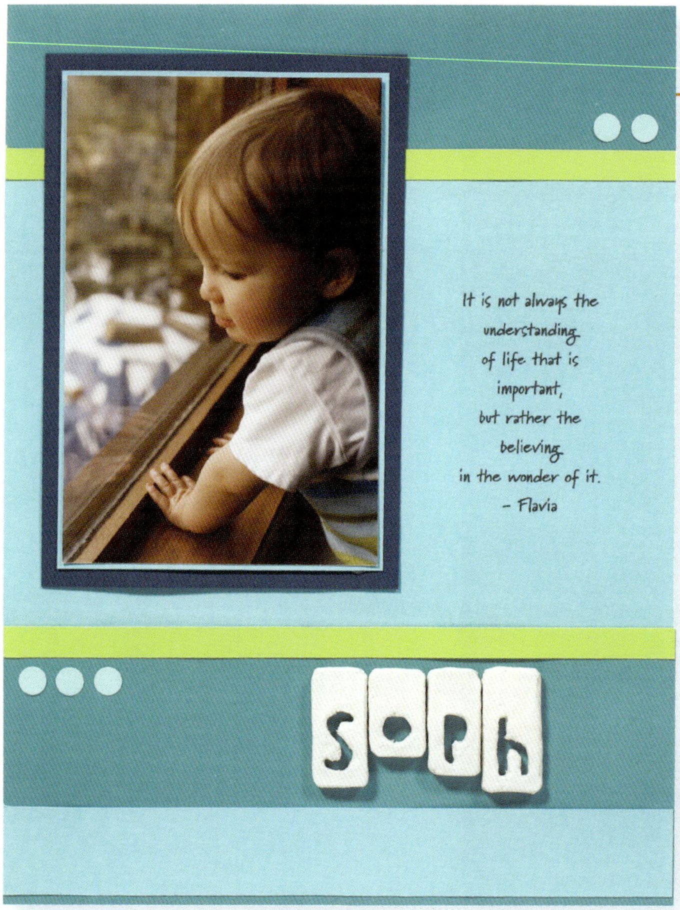

★ Vivian Smith created negative letters by making clay tiles and then cutting letters out of them with a metal embossing stylus. The clay was left uncolored to stand out against the background.

Sources: Computer font is Marydale downloaded off the Internet. Design by Vivian Smith.

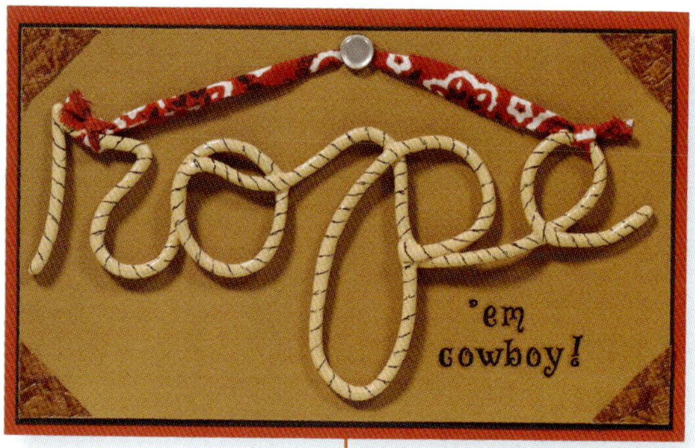

★ Sara used a clay gun for her ropelike lettering. She created a single long strand, smoothing the edges with wet fingertips. Working quickly, she spelled out the word "rope," dabbing overlapped areas with water. Once dry, the rough edges were sanded and the piece was painted with acrylic paint and clear gloss. She added details with a pen.

Sources: Textured paper by European Papers. Alphabet stickers by Provo Craft. Pen is a Slick Writer by American Crafts. Pearl button by Prym-Dritz. Design by Sara Tumpane.

To get a good impression in your clay, items with a subtle texture (such as carpet or leather, for example) will need to be pressed into the clay using more weight than a deeply textured item. Once your clay has been given a texture, allow it to dry thoroughly before you do further embellishing.

Anything Goes

Once you feel comfortable with rolling out your clay and pressing things into it for texture, try making free-form creations. If you've ever made free-form shapes with leftover rolled-cookie dough, you can make free-form paper clay accents. Here are some techniques to get you started.

Try using a kitchen knife to cut out a football shape. When dry, paint it brown with white laces and you've got the perfect embellishment for a football practice or homecoming game page. Lay one of your favorite paper die cuts (such as a leaf, star, fish, cloud, water splat, dog bone, or flower) on your rolled clay and lightly trace around it with a pencil, embossing stylus, toothpick, or knife; then cut it out. Once dry, the piece can be finished with paint, ink, or chalk.

Consider embellishments based in nature. Flowers, water droplets, rays to accompany a sun die cut, seagulls, rocks, or clouds are all easy items to form by hand. Remember, things in nature have irregular edges, so there's no need for perfection. When your creation is dry, you can always sand it to refine its shape to your liking.

Rolling a long strand of clay makes a great snake. A free-form, flat oval can be painted solid and attached to fibers or wire for dimensional birthday balloons or decorated with stripes and dots for Easter eggs.

You can take the simplest of shapes (like a circle) and transform it into a sports ball, Christmas tree ornament, bathtime bubbles, snowball, sun, clock face, smiley face, button, ladybug, beach ball, or scoop of ice cream just by the way you decorate it.

Creating free-form graphic elements for your pages gives you endless possibilities, whether simple or intricate, large or small, realistic or abstract. You can make anything you want to suit your page design.

To the Letter

Looking for new lettering options? Wait until you see what you can do with paper clay. Use it to create large title letters, letter tiles, or tiny word charms. Adding the dimension of

* Jodi Sanford used a rubber stamp to make a star impression in paper clay for this card accent. She cut a square from a thin sheet of paper clay and pressed the stamp into the surface, leaving four impressions behind. Once dry, she chalked the piece with brown crafting chalk to give it a slightly aged look and then added a raffia bow to the corner.

Sources: Patterned paper by Making Memories. Computer font is Metallic Avocado downloaded off the Internet. Rubber stamp by Westwater Enterprises. Design by Jodi Sanford.

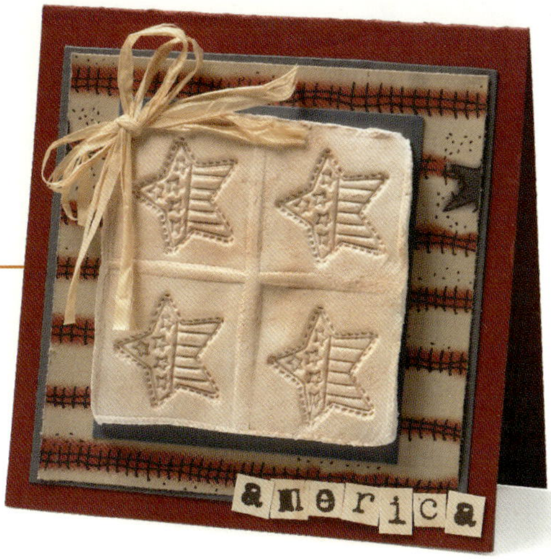

* Colleen Macdonald designed this delicate Chinese fan by pressing a rubber stamp into a rolled-out piece of clay about 1/8 inch thick and cutting around the stamped image in a softly curving shape. She also made a small hole in the bottom of the piece to attach the tassel. Once dry, the piece was painted with various colors of Radiant Pearls and then burnished with metallic rub-ons.

Sources: Radiant Pearls by Angelwings Enterprises. Rubber stamps by Denami Design (fan), All Night Media (Chinese coin), and Magenta Rubber Stamps (Chinese character). Design by Colleen Macdonald.

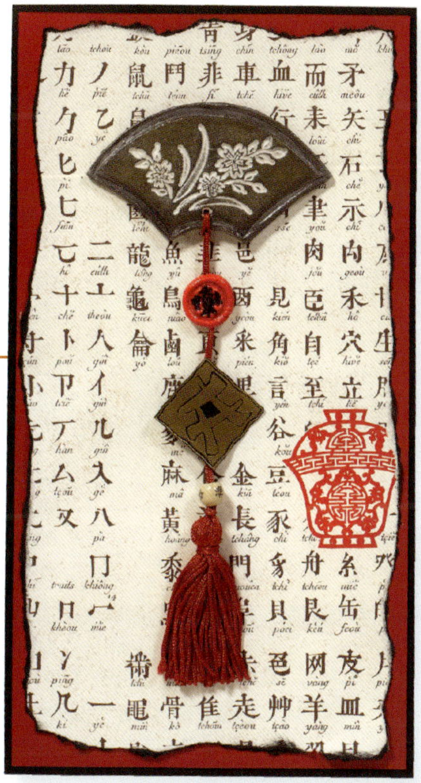

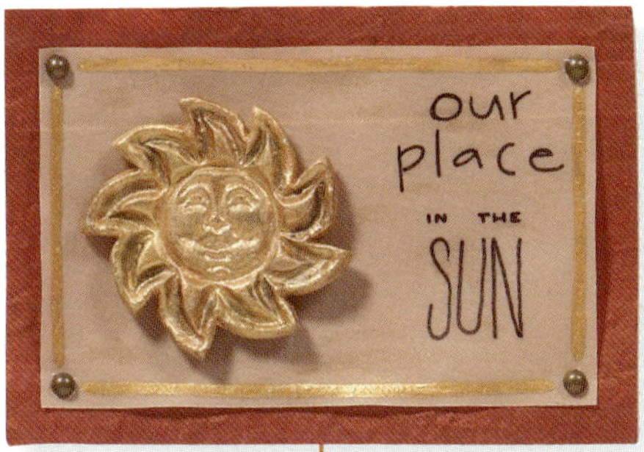

* Sara used an uninked rubber stamp to impress the sun image into damp, rolled clay. Once the clay shape was dry, she painted it with a mixture of liquid gum arabic and Pearl Ex pigment powder, and worked metallic rub-ons into the crevices and raised areas.

Sources: Rubber stamp by Stampin' Up!. Pearl Ex by Jacquard Products. Metallic rub-ons by Craf-T Products. Design by Sara Tumpane.

paper clay allows you to make certain letters or words stand out. Try using lettering templates to create clay letters. (You can use this technique with shape templates as well.) Roll the paper clay out in a thin sheet and gently press the template into the clay to create the outline of each letter. Use a knife or scissors to cut out the letters. This technique works best with template letters that are not overly ornate. Allow your letters to dry and sand the rough edges. Color the letters with chalk, ink, pigment powders, or paints, or precolor the clay by kneading in a few drops of crafts paint or ink before cutting the letters. *Note:* Wear plastic gloves for this step. It's messy!

There are other ways to use paper clay for lettering. Try using the clay gun to produce long coils of clay that can be formed into letters or use clay to create small word and letter charms. Simply stamp or write the word you need in damp clay and allow the piece to dry. Once finished, these become perfect personalized accents for your page in a very trendy style.

Are you still thinking that including paper clay designs on your pages is beyond your reach? Or are you tempted to give it a try? I hope you'll open a pack and enjoy the endless possibilities for your scrapbook pages. I know you'll come to love it as one of your scrapbooking staples. ||||

true colors

Hand tinting turns photographs of the way our world truly appears into works of interpretive art.

by Erin Terrell

As much as I love the vibrancy of color photographs, I still miss the good old days when black-and-white images reigned supreme and color was added with an artist's brush. If you, too, love the nostalgia of hand-tinted pictures, you'll welcome the diversity they can bring to your scrapbook pages.

Planning Your Shot

Before you can begin hand tinting, you need to round up the right supplies. I use Marshall's Oils for most of my hand-coloring work (see the photos *opposite*), and on *page 17* you'll find information on some of the other photo-tinting products on the market. But no matter what products you use to tint your pictures, you must start with a quality photograph. That means a well-thought-out composition with crisp contrast, a nice tonal range, and an uncluttered background.

Black-and-white photos range in tone from nearly pure white to pure black with shades of gray in between. A properly exposed and printed image will have a good balance of light and dark tones, which creates the illusion of depth.

Even though you're taking a black-and-white photograph, you still should choose your background colors and your subject's clothing with care. Avoid dark colors such as navy, burgundy, and hunter green—they'll appear black in your photos. Also avoid whites or extremely light colors. Midtones accept color the best. Have your subjects wear light-colored denim or pastel clothing. You also may want to suggest that they wear solid-color clothing, since intricate patterns and plaids are more difficult to hand-tint.

Your subjects will stand out more if you choose a simple background or keep your range of focus narrow and leave the background fuzzy. Try going outdoors to take your black-and-white photos—nature usually provides an excellent backdrop!

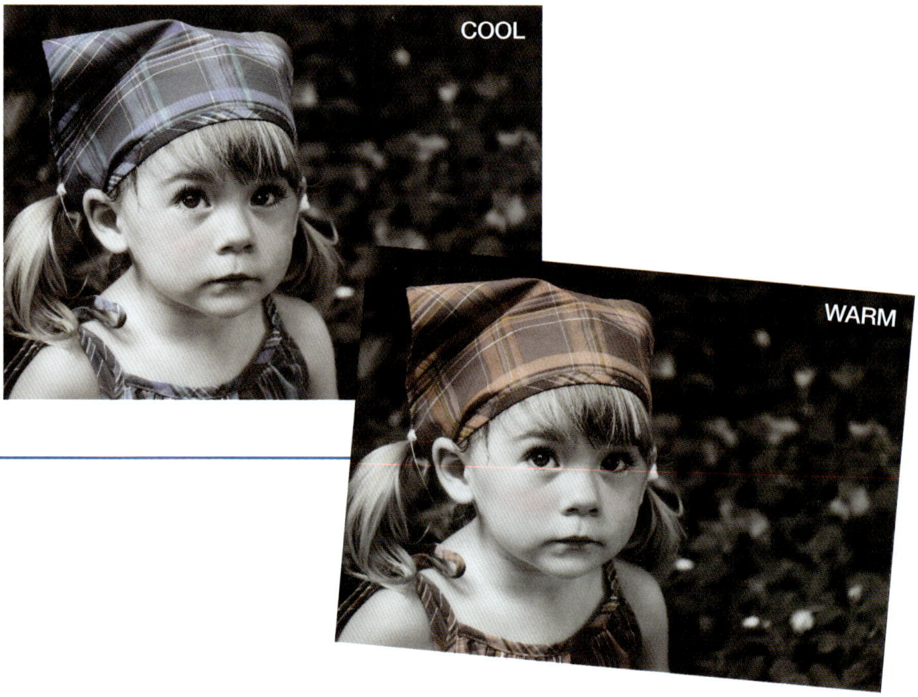

★ Erin used warm colors to tint one copy of the photo and cool tones to tint the other. Simply changing the colors of an image alters the feeling the image evokes.

Negative Thoughts

The film you choose also will affect your hand-tinting results. Although there are a number of black-and-white films available, they all fall into two distinct categories: those that use C-41 processing and those dubbed "true" black-and-white films.

Films that require C-41 processing are developed using the same equipment and techniques as color film, so they can be dropped off at nearly any commercial photo lab. Prints usually are less expensive than those produced from true black-and-white films, and the processing usually takes less time. However, prints from C-41 films don't have the crispness of true black-and-white prints. They also often exhibit a slight color tint—sepia (light brown), pink, or green.

Prints from true black-and-white films will have a crisp contrast rather than the flat gray tones that sometimes occur with C-41-processed films. Unfortunately, because professional photo shops typically are the only ones that process true black-and-white film in-house, getting prints can be more expensive than color prints or C-41-processed black-and-whites. And if you take your film to a shop that can't process it in-house, you may have to wait a bit longer for your prints because they'll send it to another lab.

Even if you've never shot black-and-white film before and aren't all that eager to try it, give hand coloring a try. You can convert your color photographs to black-and-white at most professional photo developers. Just give them the negative and ask them to make a print. And hand tinting isn't just for black-and-white prints. You also can have your photos developed with a sepia tone to give them an old-fashioned feel.

Whether you choose sepia-tone or black-and-white prints, tell the lab technician that you'll be hand-tinting the prints and would like them printed a shade or two lighter. This will ensure that the colors will show up well and the end result won't look too dark or heavy. *Note:* Do not tint a one-of-a-kind print or any print for which you don't have a negative. Go to a professional lab and have a negative made from your original print.

Perfect Prints

Just as important to the quality of your print as the type of film you use is the paper it's printed on. There are two families of photographic paper: resin-coated (RC) and fiber-based (FB).

Most commercial photo labs use RC paper which comes in two finishes: matte and glossy (some labs may offer a pearl or satin finish, but it is rare). Request a matte finish for hand tinting.

Fiber-based paper has a bit of "tooth" to it and readily accepts tinting oils. You'll need to go to a professional lab for FB paper, and you can expect to pay more for it. However, FB paper is truly archival and will last for hundreds of years with proper care.

When you first start hand coloring, think big—bigger prints, that is. Working with a 5×7-inch or an 8×10-inch print is ideal because the details will be larger and easier to see. A professional lab also can create a negative from a finished hand-tinted photo, which means you can order reprints in whatever sizes you'd like. You also can tint a large photo and then reduce it in size on a Kodak Picture Maker machine. (This is an easy way to make multiple copies of a hand-tinted photo and is great for personalizing Christmas cards.)

Color Your World

Now that you know how to shoot great photographs to work with, you're ready to start the tinting process. *Note:* I used Marshall's Oils to tint most of these examples and to describe general tinting techniques.

Your first decision is how much color you'd like to apply to your photo. It's an artistic decision and entirely up to you. Tint the whole photo, a section, or just one element.

Until you've found your hand-coloring niche, try duplicating the colors from the original photo setting. But one of the benefits of tinting is the artistic freedom it affords—you're not bound by the confines of reality!

1
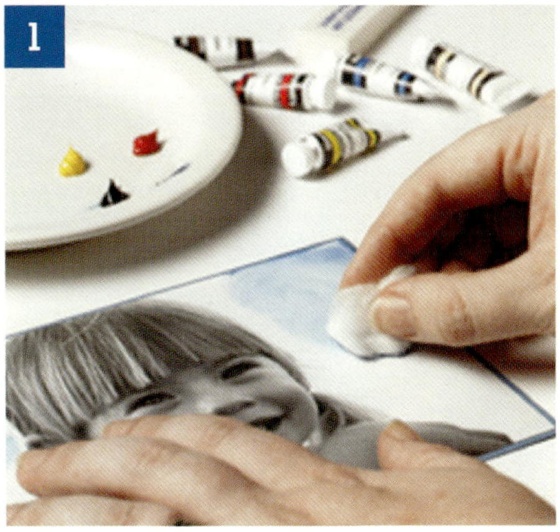

2
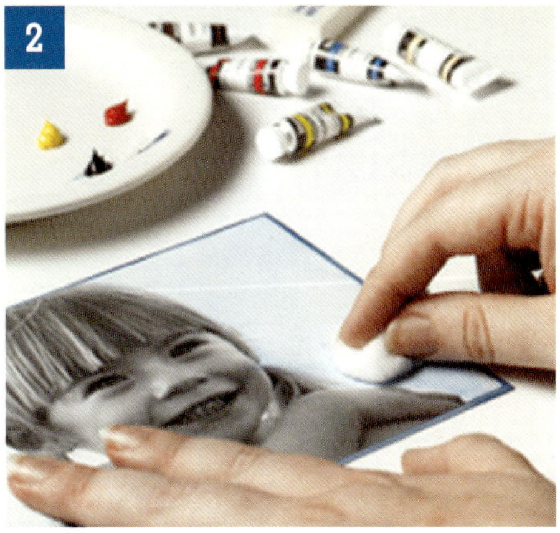

3
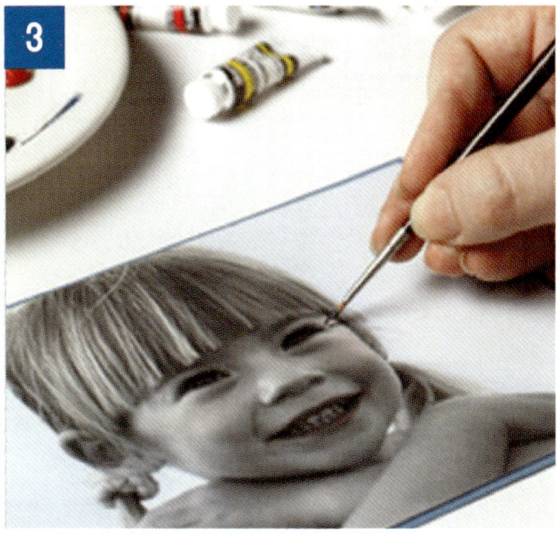

Begin by squeezing tiny amounts of the oils onto a palette or a piece of waxed paper. Apply color to the upper portion of the photo so you can rest your hand on the print without smearing it (see Photo 1, *above*). Use cotton balls to apply color to large areas, then fill in small areas with cotton swabs. Rub in a circular motion, using just enough color to lightly cover the image. It's best to apply the oils

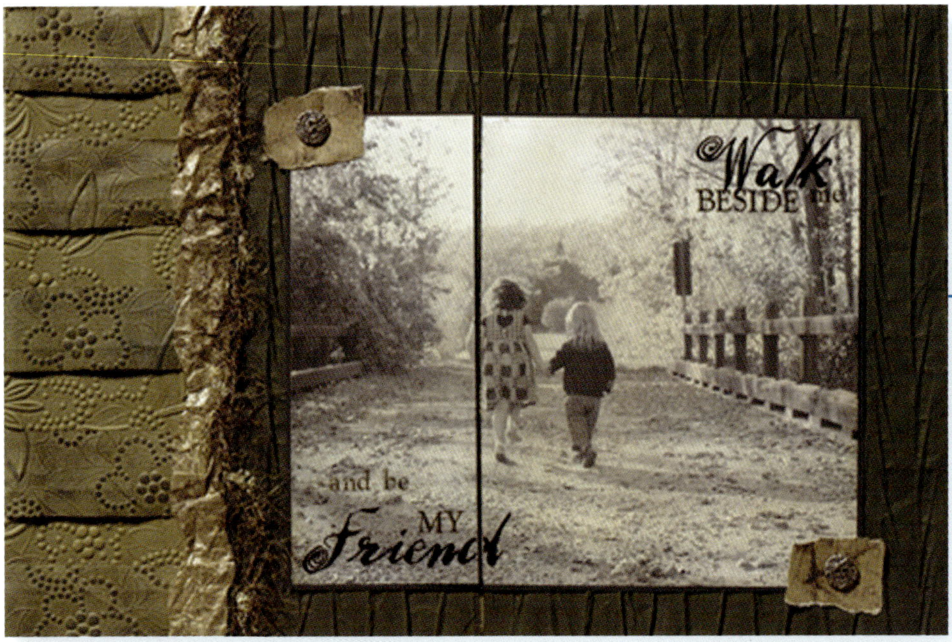

★ Danelle Johnson used Marshall's Oils to give the black-and-white photo in this layout a light green wash. It gives the image a vintage look and matches the warm tones of the papers.

Sources: Textured paper by Solum World Papers. Letter stickers by Mrs. Grossman's and by Flavia for Colorbök. Buttons by JHB International. Fibers by Rubba Dub Dub. Design by Danelle Johnson.

lightly at first. Once the print dries, you can always go back and add more color if you'd like a stronger effect.

Use a clean cotton ball to blend the color and wipe away any excess (see Photo 2, *page 15*). You want only a small amount of color to remain on the photo. When you blend the color, the longer you rub and the harder you press, the lighter the color becomes. So use a light, delicate touch at first. If the color doesn't lighten sufficiently, bear down a little more. Thoroughly blend each area before coloring adjacent areas.

Marshall's Oils are transparent; photograph details will always show through. This makes shading and highlighting almost unnecessary.

Another neat feature of these oils is that when two colors overlap, the second color usually will remove all traces of the first color. So, if an oil color bleeds into an area that you haven't yet tinted, simply apply the new color. In most cases, the unwanted color will disappear (yellow over blue is the only exception).

But as convenient as this process can be, it also makes mixing colors a bit tricky. Don't try mixing colors right on the photograph. Instead, mix them on a palette before you apply them. If a color seems too bold or bright, mix it with a little bit of extender to lighten the tint. You can darken a color by adding a neutral tint. For pastel colors, mix the base color with white oil.

To add the smallest details to your photograph, work with a fine artist's brush (see Photo 3, *page 15*).

You Can't Go Wrong

It's practically impossible to make mistakes when you hand-color with Marshall's Oils. They take at least 24 hours to dry, so you'll have plenty of time to make corrections and fine-tune. If you aren't happy with the color you've applied, simply wipe it off with a clean cotton cloth and try something new.

There also are ways to remove stubborn colors. PM Solution is an oil-based medium you can use to clean fingerprints off your print before hand tinting as well as to remove unwanted color. Marlene is an alcohol-based cleaner that works in much the same way. But perhaps the easiest way to remove unwanted color from a photograph is with a white nonabrasive eraser (included in some Marshall's sets or available separately).

On a portrait, you can use the eraser to remove color from the whites of the eyes or from teeth, as well as to clean up the edges if you've colored "outside the lines."

If you have to stop before you finish tinting a print, simply make sure you've erased any stray oil marks from the edges of the completed section, and that you're happy with the colors you've applied, since they'll dry that way. Then you can return days or weeks later to finish your print.

Hand-tinted prints will take anywhere from 24 hours to a few weeks to dry. The drying time depends on how thickly you've applied the oils, the paper your photo was printed on, and the level of humidity in the air. To speed the drying time, you can mix equal parts of Marshall's Drier with the oils on your palette, and your prints will dry in approximately 6 hours.

I hope the layouts shown here inspire you to give hand coloring a try. And if you keep these tips and techniques in mind, you can proceed with confidence. Have fun, and enjoy the one-of-a-kind prints you create!

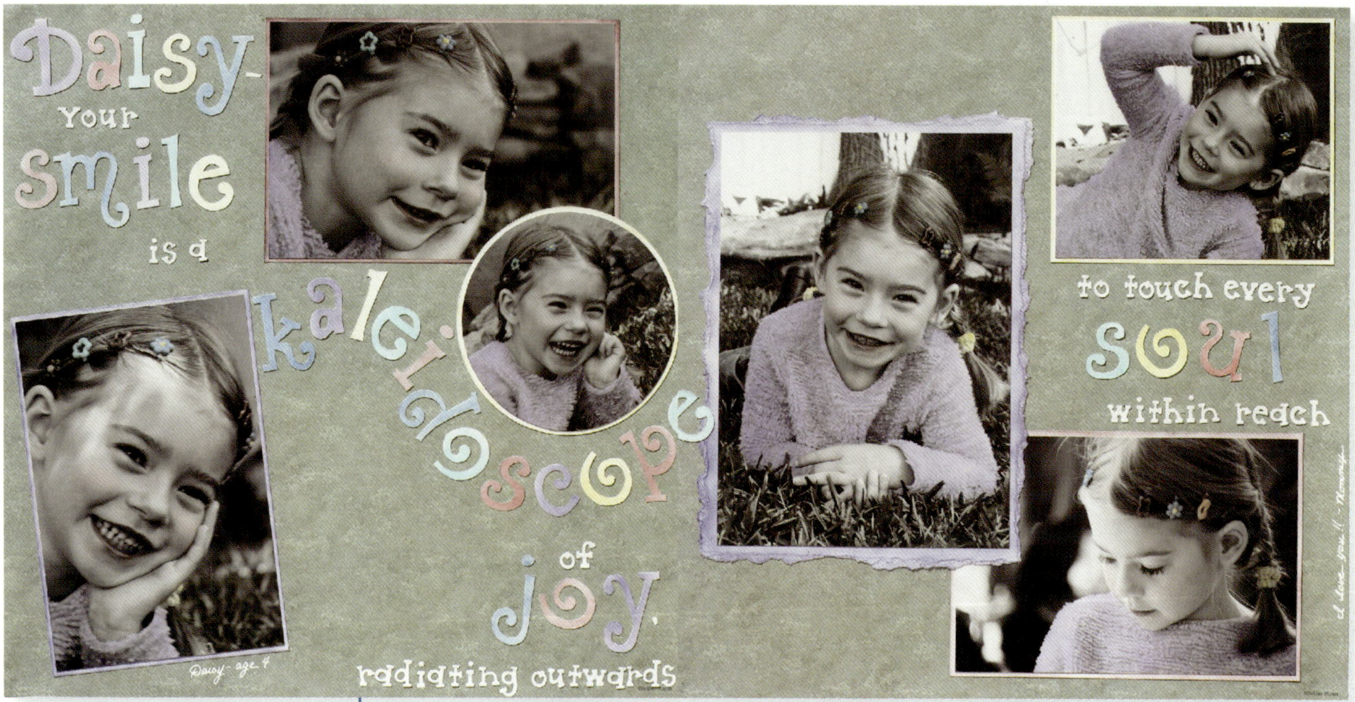

★ Since Marshall's Oils are photo-safe, you can use them to create colorful titles and embellishments on your pages. Here, Erin used a cotton ball to wipe the oil onto letters cut from acid-free card stock, adhering them to the page when they were dry.

Sources: Patterned paper by Debbie Mumm. Alphabitties stickers by Provo Craft. Curly Q lettering template by ScrapPagerz. Design by Erin Terrell.

EXPLORE YOUR OPTIONS

	Marshall's Oils	Creative Photo Tinting Dyes	Prismacolor Pencils	EK Success Photo Twins	Spot Pens
Can it color on matte-finish photos?	Y	Y	Y	Y	Y With advance surface preparation
Can it color on glossy-finish photos?	Y With advance surface preparation	Y	N	Y	Y With advance surface preparation
Can it color on Kodak Picture Maker prints?	Y With advance surface preparation	N	N	N	N
Can you blend the colors?	Y	Y	Y	N	N
Can you layer color to make it darker?	Y	Y	Y To some degree	Y	Y
Can you lighten color if you apply too much?	Y	Y	Y	Y	Y
Can you remove color if you make a mistake?	Y	Y May not be able to remove all the color	Y	N	N
How long does it take to dry?	Varies (hours to days)	Minutes	Instant	30 minutes	1 hour
Does it come with an instructional video or booklet?	Both—for additional cost	Yes—booklet included	No	No	Video—at additional cost

by the book

The art of creating altered books can unleash your artistic impulses and make memory albums worthy of display.

by Alison Beachem

I remember my first experience with scrapbooking at a friend's home party. I obediently followed all the instructions I was given until the instructor told me to cut my photos. Was she crazy?

Letting Go

I had a similar reaction when I sat down to make my first altered book, a fabulous art form popular with collage and stamping artists. From my earliest memories I had been told not to cut or mark in books—something I've told my own children time and time again. But the temptation can prove too great. I often find a squiggle here, a doodle there. So, I pushed aside my adult ideas about writing in books (as I did my fears about cropping scrapbook photos) and gave way to the inner, creative child.

What is an altered book? Basically it's an old book that has been altered—painted, cut, stamped, glued, colored, whatever—and transformed into your own work of art. Altered books generally involve a lot of collage art and usually pull from the stamping and painting arenas. But you needn't stop there! Creating an altered book is the perfect excuse to try all the techniques and products you've wanted to use in scrapbooking but have been reluctant to try. If you've never used eyelets and have a few lying around, add eyelets to a page. Have you ever wanted to try embossing powders on your scrapbook pages but were afraid of mucking everything up? Try it in your altered book and let your mistakes become "creative accents." When you find a look you like, transfer the technique to your other crafts.

You can create a personal journal out of an old book. Write your daily thoughts on different pages. Add your own doodles and drawings alongside writings that reflect your mood. Use a color that represents how you are feeling, or add bits of memorabilia that

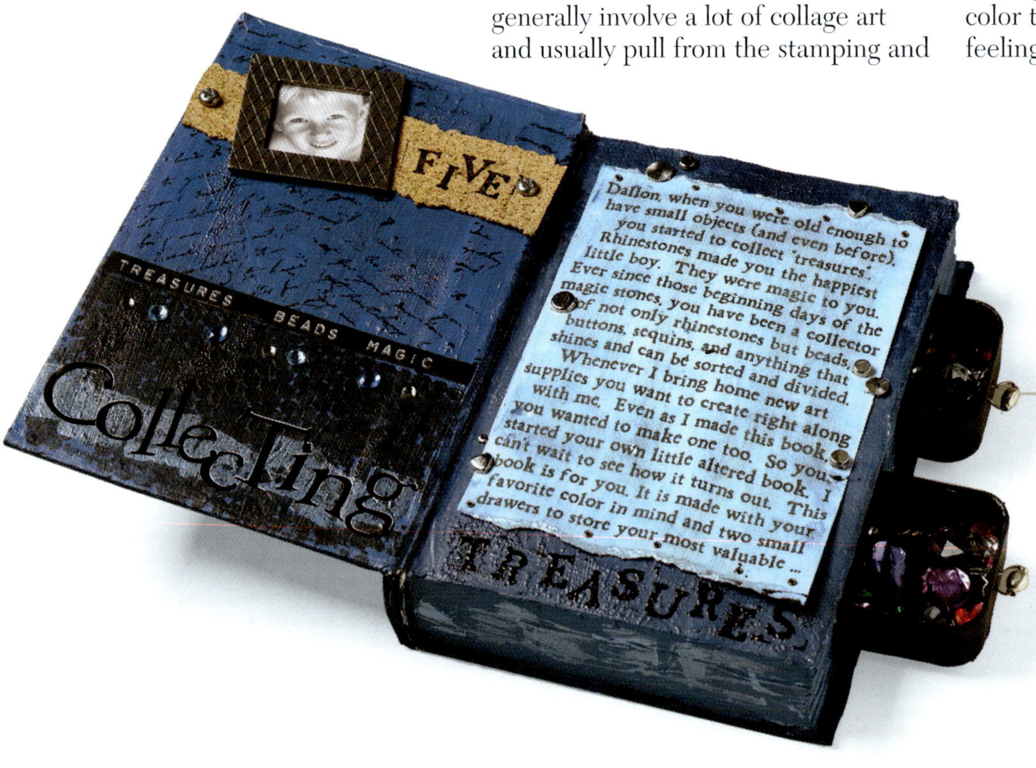

★ Alison keeps notes filled with scrapbooking ideas, and her son's obsession with treasures is one that has stumped her for a long time. While researching altered books for this article, Alison stumbled across the idea of creating drawers in books with empty mint tins. She traced the tins and cut out the spaces with a crafts knife. Then she covered the tins with acrylic gesso. Once dry, she painted the book and then added stamps, cork, eyelets, and a message to her son.

Sources: Computer font is Sleigh Ride by Twopeasinabucket.com. Alphabet stickers by Sonnets for Creative Imaginations. Rubber stamps by Hero Arts (square block), The Missing Link (alphabet), and Fishbone Graphics (script). Metal frame, screw snaps, and minieyelets by Making Memories. Label maker by Dymo. Design by Alison Beachem.

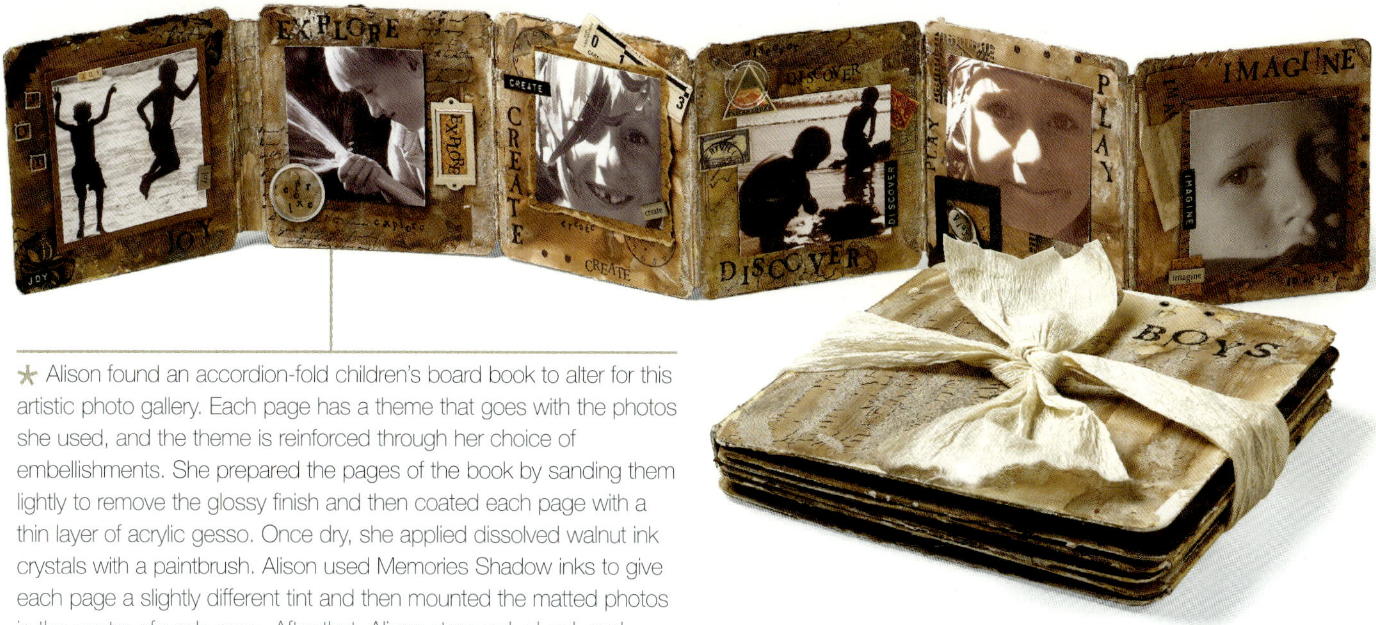

★ Alison found an accordion-fold children's board book to alter for this artistic photo gallery. Each page has a theme that goes with the photos she used, and the theme is reinforced through her choice of embellishments. She prepared the pages of the book by sanding them lightly to remove the glossy finish and then coated each page with a thin layer of acrylic gesso. Once dry, she applied dissolved walnut ink crystals with a paintbrush. Alison used Memories Shadow inks to give each page a slightly different tint and then mounted the matted photos in the center of each page. After that, Alison stamped, glued, and attached items until she had embellished each page to her satisfaction.

Sources: Faux leather trim by Crafters Toybox. Label maker by Dymo. Rubber stamps by Provo Craft (shell), The Missing Link (alphabet), PSX (alphabet), Hero Arts (alphabet and square), Inkadinkado (clock), Stampa Rosa (map), and Fishbone Graphics (script). Metal words, snaps, eyelets, oval picture pebble, and vellum tag by Making Memories. Typewriter key letters by Artchix Studio. Design by Alison Beachem.

will remind you of the day's events. You also can construct theme books just as you would theme albums. Friends would love to receive a book of photos from their wedding (or some other event) that serves as a work of art as well as a record of the occasion.

Whether you choose to make a book to document a happening much like a scrapbook or simply to unleash your artistic impulses, you'll find that an altered book is a great way to bring added creativity to your life. So, let your guard down and start snipping.

Getting Started

First, find a book to alter. Choose one that sparks a memory, recounts an event, raises a question, or speaks to you in some way. You can even use a book that just ties in with the embellishments you have on hand. The cover or texture of a book may intrigue you as well. Old travel books or atlases may be perfect for showcasing vacation memorabilia in a unique way. An inspirational book may have words in it that guide your design. A botanical book could be the perfect choice to display photos of your garden. If you have a theme in mind and can't find a book to match, don't worry: You can mask all the text with paints or inks!

Hardcover books or children's board books work best. You'll need a book that can handle being cut and glued. You can find old books at thrift stores for a dollar or two, and libraries often sell old books for next to nothing. Ask friends if they have old books they'd like to get rid of, or you may even have a few books of your own that will fit your needs. My favorite choices for altering are children's board books. They're sturdy and have a limited number of pages, so they work well for constructing small theme projects.

Remember, there is no right way to create an altered book: Glue pages together; cut out a niche or window; fold or tear pages; create pockets or peekaboo pages. Use whatever supplies you wish. Break out the crayons, poster paints, or other art supplies lurking at the bottom of your crafting closet. Cut out pictures from old magazines. Photocopy or computer-print photographs. Gather memorabilia that are meaningful but don't have a place elsewhere. And don't forget your handy cache of scrapbooking supplies.

Basic Techniques

Once you have a book and a theme, determine how many pages you want to alter. The pages of a typical book generally are not sturdy enough to hold embellishments or to be painted on, so you'll need to glue pages together for strength. Depending on the thickness of the individual pages and the effect you're after, you can glue as few as two or as many as several hundred pages at a time.

The type of glue you use will affect the appearance of your altered book. Use one that doesn't buckle the pages. I like Lineco Neutral pH Adhesive. You also can try Perfect Paper Adhesive or Yes! Glue. Another good choice is Polyvinyl Acetate Adhesive by Volcano Book Arts. Use a heavy piece of card stock, chipboard, or an old credit card to smooth out the glue and spread it evenly over the pages. Once the pages are glued together, set something heavy on top of your book while it dries.

If you want to adhere all the pages together, use a product such as artists'

by the book

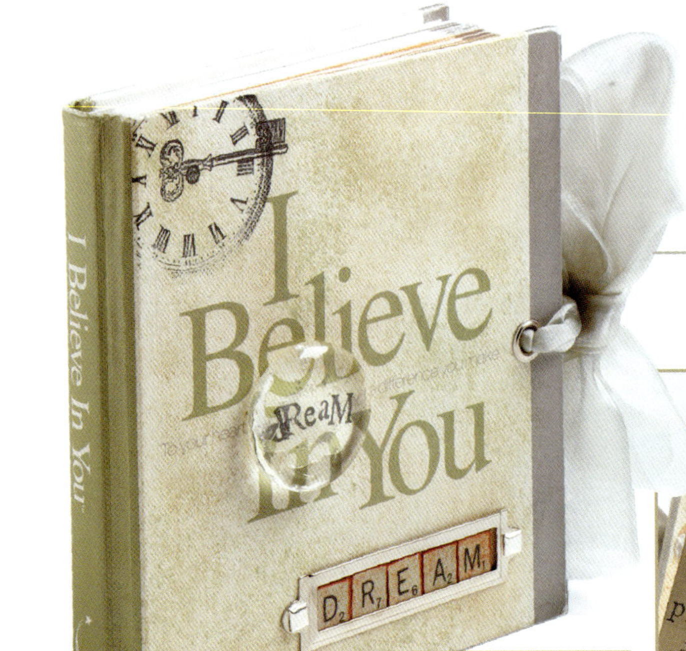

★ Nichol Magouirk constructed this book about believing in her dreams and goals by altering a book of inspirational quotes. She modified the cover of the book only a little, adding a stamped image and word, then accentuating the word with a large glass page pebble. She also used Scrabble tile letters to spell out the word "Dream," which she framed with a bookplate. Nichol used a combination of walnut ink and stamping ink to tint the pages, allowing the original text on the pages to peek through. She glued the bulk of the pages together in the back of the book, which allowed her to cut a deep shadow box for displaying a glass case with a tiny silver poetry charm inside. Other pages are decorated with stamped images, found objects, postage stamps, and vintage photos.

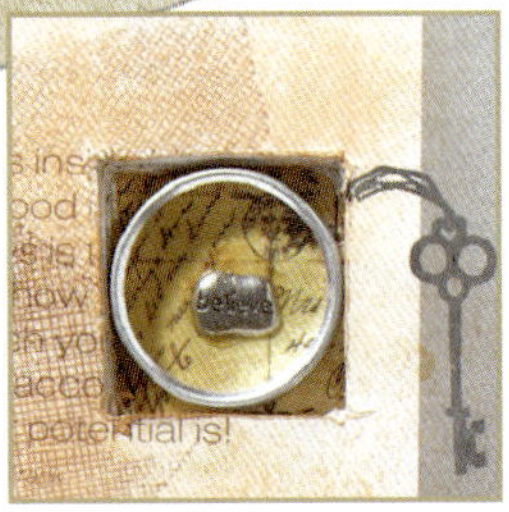

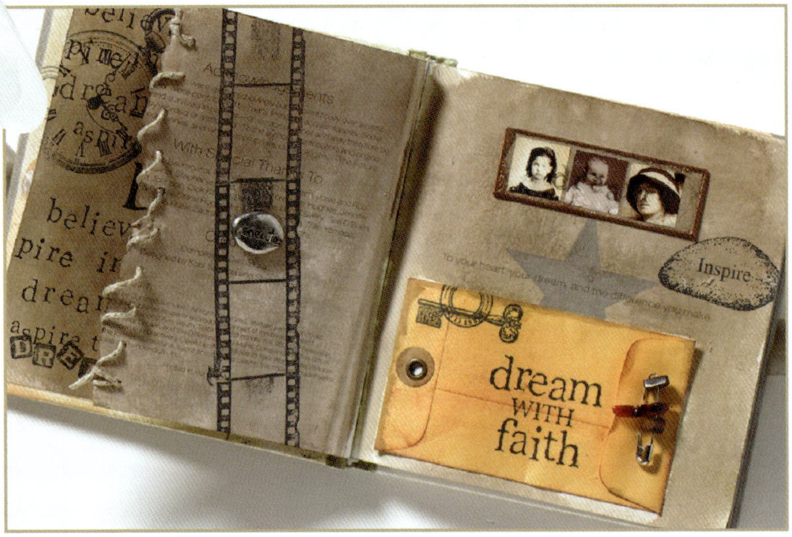

Sources: Rubber stamps by PSX (alphabet), Uptown Design (dream in blocks), Stamp of Excellence (handwritten background), Inkadinkado (clock, film strip, "inspire," "believe," and "dream with faith"), Magenta Rubber Stamps (keys), Diffusion ("inspire" and "dream" in stones), and Hero Arts (crosshatch background and postage stamp). Walnut ink by Anima Designs. Picture pebble by Magic Scraps. Scrabble tile letters by Limited Edition Rubber Stamps. Bookplate, poetry charm, and tags by Twopeasinabucket.com. Transparency, vintage photos, letters, glass slide, and postage stamps by Stampington & Co. Watch crystal by Deluxe Plastic Arts. Minibrads by Lost Art Treasures. Design by Nichol Magouirk.

acrylic gesso. Open the front cover and apply the gesso with a paintbrush along the sides and under the back cover. Lay something heavy on top of the book to keep it flat. As it dries, you may want to add more gesso on the sides to fill in any pockets. This will take a day to dry.

Other methods of securing pages together don't require any adhesive. For just a few pages at a time, try using eyelets or brads. Or try piercing holes in each corner and running wire down through the pages. Break out the power tools and use a drill to make holes in the book; then secure the pages with screws. Experiment and find out what works best for you and the project you're tackling.

Niches or compartments for three-dimensional objects are very popular in altered books. To cut out a niche, decide on its shape and depth. Draw the shape on the top page where you want the niche. Adhere the pages together using one of the methods mentioned above. If you glue pages together, do this before you cut. After the pages dry, use a utility or crafts knife to cut out the niche. If you use gesso, trace the pattern and then cut it out. Once you have finished cutting, apply gesso on the sides and bottom of the niche and let it dry.

The cover can be the most intriguing part of your altered book and presents unlimited possibilities. Use lots of embellishments for flair, or downplay it with just a title and a few accents. How about putting a window in the cover that gives viewers a peek of what's inside? It's really quite simple. Create a template for the desired shape of your window and trace it on the front cover. Use a utility or crafts knife to cut it out. You can place a piece of transparency, vellum, or plastic behind the window, or leave it open for a dimensional object to show through.

Applying the Techniques Elsewhere

Altered book techniques don't have to stay within altered books. Incorporate these ideas into your scrapbooking designs (see the examples *opposite*).

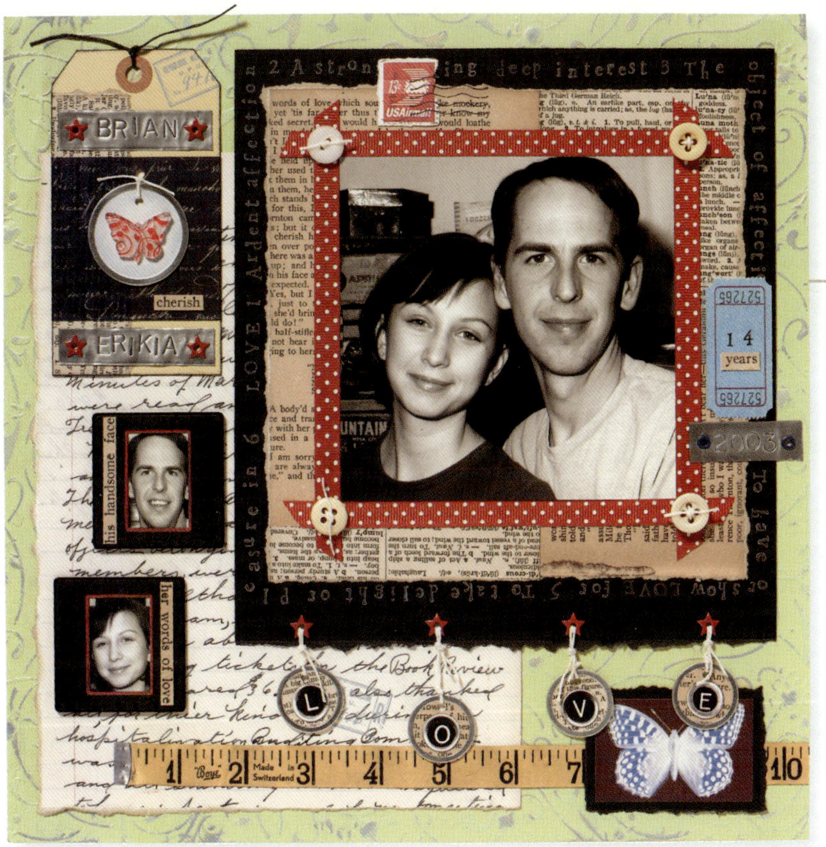

★ Designer Erikia Ghumm adapted the altered book techniques and philosophy to work on a scrapbook page, a journal cover, and a card. For the page, Erikia added interest to embossed card stock by rubbing it with ink to bring out the pattern and then layered copies of handwritten letters, torn book pages, photographs, and other memorabilia to create a page that makes a statement about the artist. To dress up a plain journal, Erikia scanned an old letter and a book cover, resized them, and printed them out. She layered the elements, adding colored rhinestones for interest. Once she was happy with the arrangement, she brushed on a coat of matte-finish acrylic sealer (by Plaid) to protect the finished product. The bow-adorned card features many of the same techniques as the journal and scrapbook page.

Sources: Page—Embossed paper by K&Company. Circle punch by Family Treasures. Metal-rim tags by Making Memories. Blue butterfly, blue text transparency, and typewriter key letters by Artchix Studio. Slide mounts by Loersch. Crafting foil by St. Louis Crafts. Rubber stamps by Hero Arts. Metal stamps by Young Bros. Stamp Works Inc. Star eyelets by JewelCraft. Album: Album by DMD. Rubber stamps by Stampers Anonymous. Metal letters and rhinestones by JewelCraft. Vintage photo of woman by Artchix Studio. Crafting foil by St. Louis Crafts. Card: Card by Hero Arts. Rubber stamps by Hero Arts (woman and alphabets). Photo corners by Canson. Vintage photo of woman by Artchix Studio. Eyelets, rhinestone, and mirrors by JewelCraft. Glitter glue by Ranger. Designs by Erikia Ghumm.

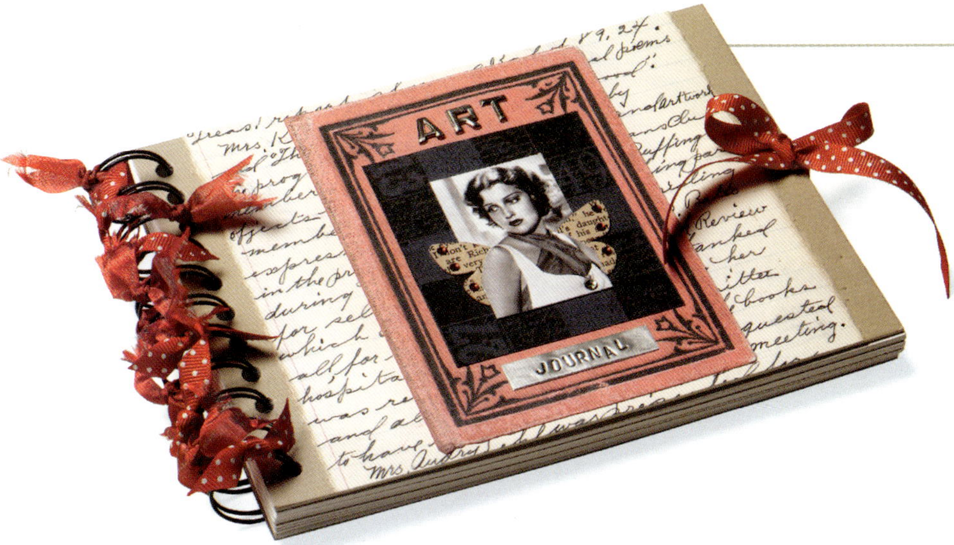

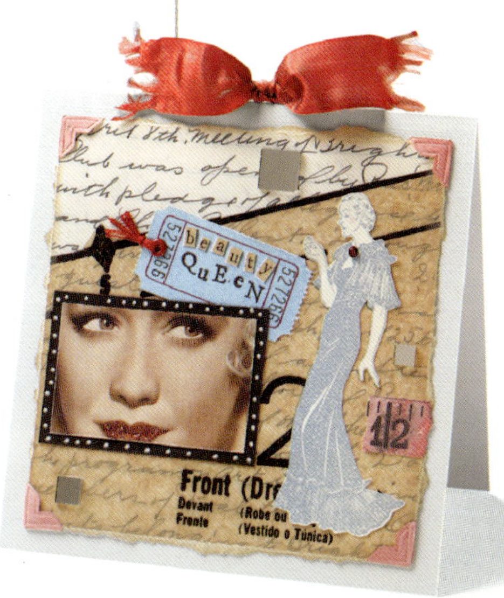

Use pages torn from an old or damaged book to create an artsy background for your photos. Create greeting cards with an altered book look. Work with collage elements to give a personal touch to the blank cover of a journal or photo album.

Altered books combine easily with the art of scrapbooking. Including memorabilia or favorite photographs will make your altered book a meaningful piece of history for you and your family. And once you start making these beautiful pieces, you won't want to stop. The only real challenge will be explaining to your little ones why you get to cut and mark in books and they can't!

imagine that

Give your scrapbook pages and other paper creations artistic flair with image-transfer techniques of all kinds.

by Erikia Ghumm

With image transfers, I can adorn nearly any surface with photographs and turn somewhat ordinary images into intricate works of art.

A New Kind of Artistry

The first hobby I was truly passionate about before scrapbooking was photography. I was captivated by the thought of being able to produce works of art without having to draw or paint them. In high school I took as many photography classes as I could, and it wasn't long after graduation that I began to yearn for my own darkroom. Luckily, my husband shared my interest and together we built one at home. Over the years we have enjoyed going on photo shoots and then coming home to develop and print our film. But eventually I found I wanted to do something more with the photographs I was including in my scrapbooks—something that would take them to the next creative level. And when I discovered the world of image transfers, I knew that was what I had been looking for.

Many different techniques and products are available to make photographic image transfers, and each will give your transferred image a different look. Although every technique has some rules that must be followed to achieve success, a high level of skill isn't required. There are basically two ways to make image transfers: using photocopied images in conjunction with typical art materials

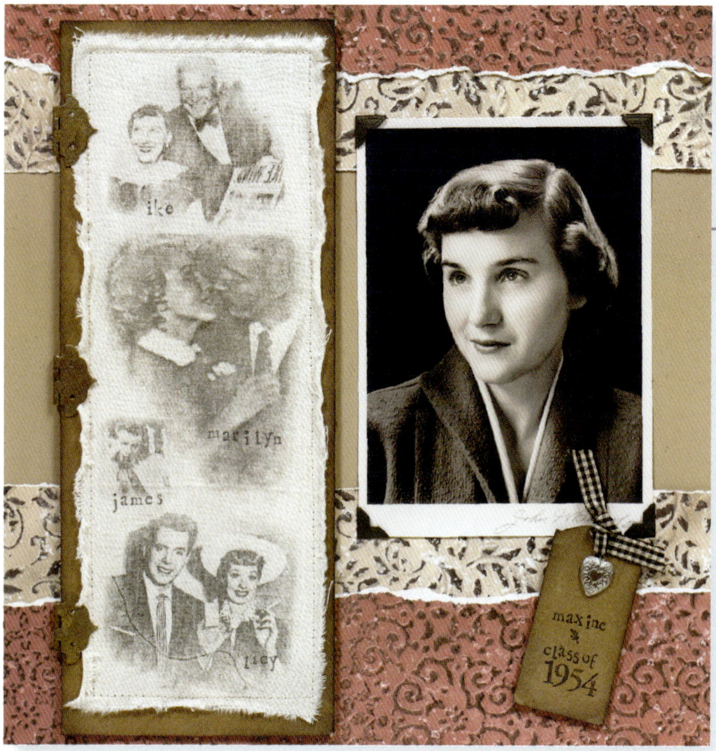

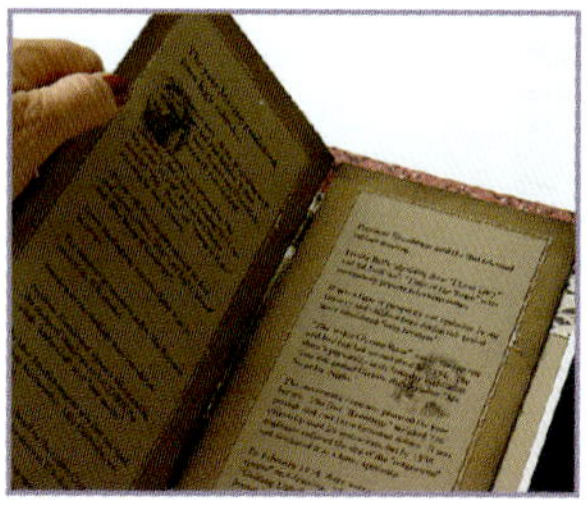

★ Polly Maly used a blender pen to transfer images copied from old magazines to the cloth cover and inside pages of the hinged book on this layout. After transferring the images, she distressed the edges of the chipboard she used to make her book covers and machine-stitched the muslin to the front. She transferred additional images to the inside card stock pages and computer-printed journaling on each. After assembling the rest of the layout, she attached the small brass hinges and secured the book to the page.

Sources: Embossed paper by Paper Adventures. Computer font is Garamouche by P22. Rubber stamps by Hero Arts (numbers) and All Night Media (alphabet). Colorless blender pen by Eberhard Faber. Photo corners by Kolo. Brass hinges from Home Depot. Ribbon by Midori. Design by Polly Maly.

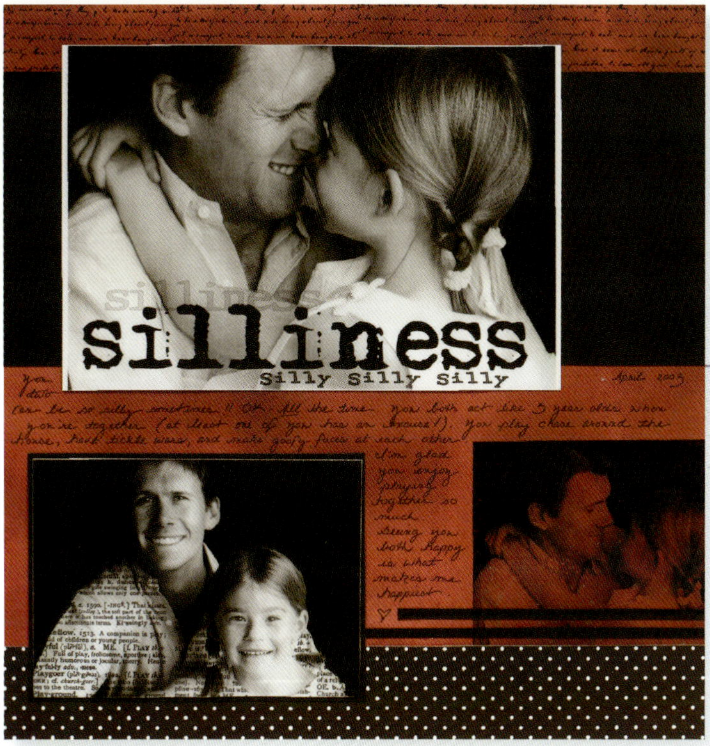

★ Erin Terrell used laminate to create see-through images on this page. On the image in the lower left corner, she positioned paper with printed dictionary definitions behind the transparent areas. The image in the right corner was adhered directly to the red background, and the main image was mounted to a piece of white paper with text printed on it.

Sources: Patterned paper by Karen Foster Design (red) and 7Gypsies (definitions). Computer fonts are Typewriter ("silly silly silly") by Elemeno and Adler (large "silliness") and Incognitype (small "silliness") downloaded off the Internet. Rubber stamp (script at top of page) by Dawn Houser for Inkadinkado. Laminate by Keep A Memory. Design by Erin Terrell.

and using specialty mediums to apply your images to various surfaces. We'll cover all the different methods here, but no matter which technique you choose, you're sure to end up with an image that will give character and interest to any design.

Transferring with Photocopies

Using a photocopier to make reproductions of your photographs is one of the simplest methods for getting your images into a form that can be used to make image transfers. It's the ideal place for beginners to start dabbling in the art. The following techniques are fairly simple and quick.

Colorless blender pens. One of the fastest and easiest ways to make a photo transfer is using a colorless blender pen. This technique allows you to reproduce your photographs onto card stock, vellum, or even fabric. The resulting image is soft and ghostly. One of my favorite ways to build on this technique is to hand-tint the transferred images with chalk or colored pencils. And because it's so simple, you can experiment with transferring your images onto different papers and using different coloring techniques.

To get started, reverse the image as you photocopy it or the final image will be backward. Place your photocopied image facedown on a sheet of card stock or vellum. You may want to tape down one side of your image using removable tape because any movement will cause a blurry transfer. Using a colorless blender pen that contains xylene, firmly color over the back of the photocopy until it is saturated. Rub the saturated image with a spoon or a burnisher to transfer the image. Carefully lift up one corner of the photocopied image to make sure it has transferred. If the transferred image isn't dark enough, color over the top of the photocopy and burnish again. Once you've achieved the desired darkness, just peel off the photocopy. It's that simple.

Laminate. Creating transfers with laminate is another simple technique. You can find laminate at most crafts and hobby stores. It comes in glossy and matte finishes and can be acid-free. (I like using Therm O Web Keep A Memory Acid Free Laminate Sheets.) With this technique, you can create a somewhat transparent and durable image that is appropriate for other crafts projects such as scrapbook covers and memory boxes.

To start the transfer process, apply laminate to the front side of a photocopied photograph. Burnish with a bone folder on the back to ensure the photocopy is adhered well to the laminate. Trim away any excess paper and laminate. Place the laminated photo into a tub of warm water for 1 to 2 minutes. When the paper is saturated, gently rub it off, leaving only the transferred image behind. Be careful to not remove too much at once or you'll get a hole in your image. Dry the transfer with a lint-free cloth. If desired, you can further manipulate the image by scratching or rubbing the edges on the back to remove more of the image. Adhere the laminate to your project with a spray or sheet adhesive such as Therm O Web Keep A Memory Acid Free Mounting Sheets.

You can achieve a similar look using clear packing tape. Apply the

imagine that

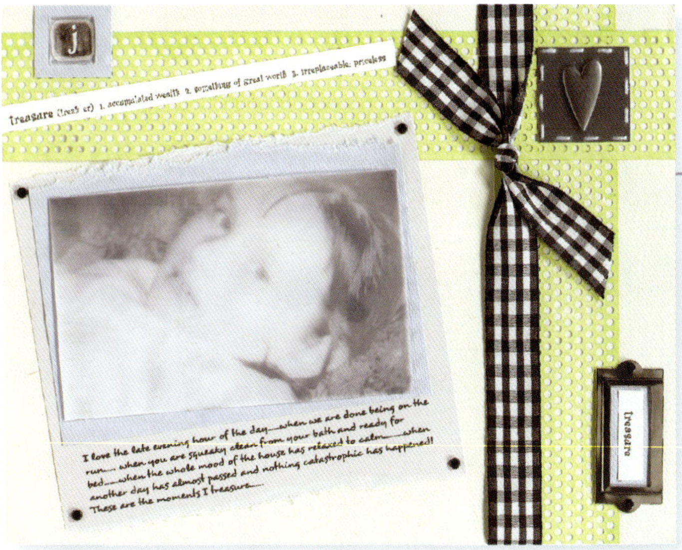

★ Kathleen Paneitz used TLS to make the thin, plasticlike image on this page. Designing her page in a landscape format, she mounted the image to a piece of light blue card stock, then adhered both pieces to a gray mat on which she had printed her journaling. Kathleen constructed an interesting background for the page by crisscrossing two strips of green mesh paper, adding a bow, and accenting with metal embellishments and a dictionary definition.

Sources: Dotted mesh paper by Magic Mesh. Computer font is Desyrel downloaded off the Internet. Translucent Liquid Sculpey by Polyform Products. Label holder and black minibrads by Magic Scraps. Sticker ("J") by Sharon Soneff for Creative Imaginations. Square page pebble, heart eyelet shape, tin tile, and dictionary definition by Making Memories. Ribbon by Offray. Design by Kathleen Paneitz.

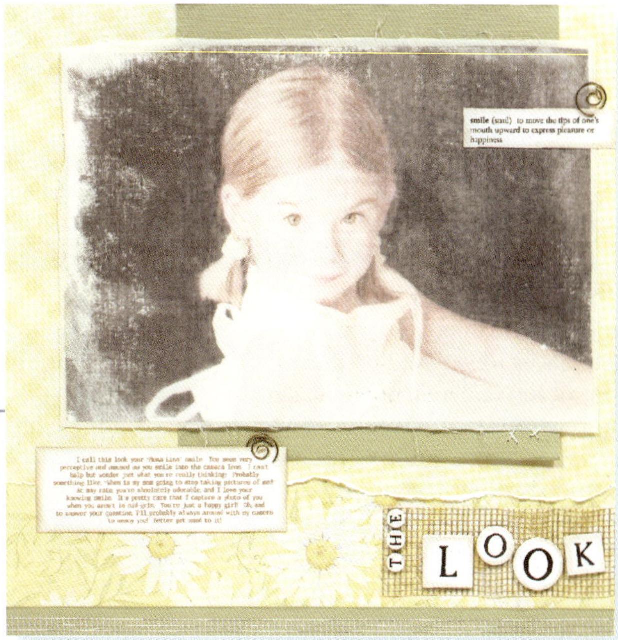

★ Erin Terrell used gel medium to transfer this color image of her daughter Daisy to a piece of light yellow cloth. Once the final coat of gel medium had been applied and dried, she used spray adhesive to attach the piece to the page background. For the page title, Erin painted metal letters with acrylic paint, inked the edges with brown ink for a less harsh appearance, and attached them with Glue Dots.

Sources: Patterned papers by K&Company. Computer font is Incognitype downloaded off the Internet. Printed dictionary definition, clips, and metal letters by Making Memories. Plastic mesh by Magic Mesh. Glue Dots by Glue Dots International. Design by Erin Terrell.

tape to a photocopied image just as you would the laminate. Soak in water and rub the paper off the back, leaving the image behind.

Liquid Sculpey (TLS). TLS is a transfer medium that can be baked and used alone or in conjunction with Sculpey polymer clay. It creates a thin, semitranslucent layer that is flexible like rubber, giving transferred photos a frosted-glass look. Purchase TLS at hobby and crafts stores that sell polymer clay. To locate a store near you, check the Web site at www.sculpey.com.

Apply a thin, even layer of TLS to a sheet of glass. Place your photocopied image facedown into the TLS (color photocopies will give a brighter, cleaner-looking transfer). Use only high-quality copy paper such as Hammermill 28 weight. Gently press the image into the TLS, starting in the center and working your way out to the edge, removing any air bubbles as you go. Allow the image to sit on the TLS for 5 minutes. In the oven, bake the glass, TLS, and paper at 275° F for 15 minutes. Remove the glass from the oven and while still hot, carefully peel the paper from the TLS. If necessary, use a crafts knife to separate the paper from the TLS. Use care as the TLS will be very hot. Once the paper has been removed and before the TLS cools completely, peel it off the glass and lay it on a smooth surface to finish cooling. You can use the transferred image as is and adhere it to heavyweight card stock with a thin layer of liquid glue. Or you can take it a step further by sculpting polymer clay into a decorative accent, adding the transfer to it by using TLS as an adhesive, and baking the entire piece according to the package instructions.

Transferring with Specialty Art Products

Using specialty art products to create photo transfers will allow you to apply images to even more surfaces. These techniques involve a little more work and products you may not be familiar with, but they will enable you to create one-of-a-kind transfers that will add a truly artistic touch to all your projects.

Gel medium. Gel medium is used by painters to extend working times in paint and by collage artists as an adhesive and a protective sealer. It can be purchased at almost any art or hobby store in the fine art paint department. (I recommend Golden Soft Gel Medium.) Using gel medium to make image transfers will give your images a rough, timeworn look. They can be transferred to any paper surface that can stand up to moisture, such as card stock, watercolor paper, or acetate.

Use an ink-jet printer to print your photograph on a piece of standard copy paper. This technique will not work with the inks in a photocopier or a laser printer. Reverse the image before printing if you don't want a mirror image of your original photo. Closeup photos or those with large subjects work best because you will lose some of the image in the transfer process. Paint a thin film of gel medium on the surface you'll be transferring the image to. Immediately place the printed image facedown onto the wet gel medium and smooth it out. Let the image sit for about 20 seconds before burnishing firmly. Peel back the top paper to check the progress of the transfer. If your image has a few holes in it, try burnishing over those areas again, or if needed, apply more gel medium only to the holes and burnish again. Once satisfied with the transfer, remove the top paper and apply a thin final coat of gel medium to seal the image.

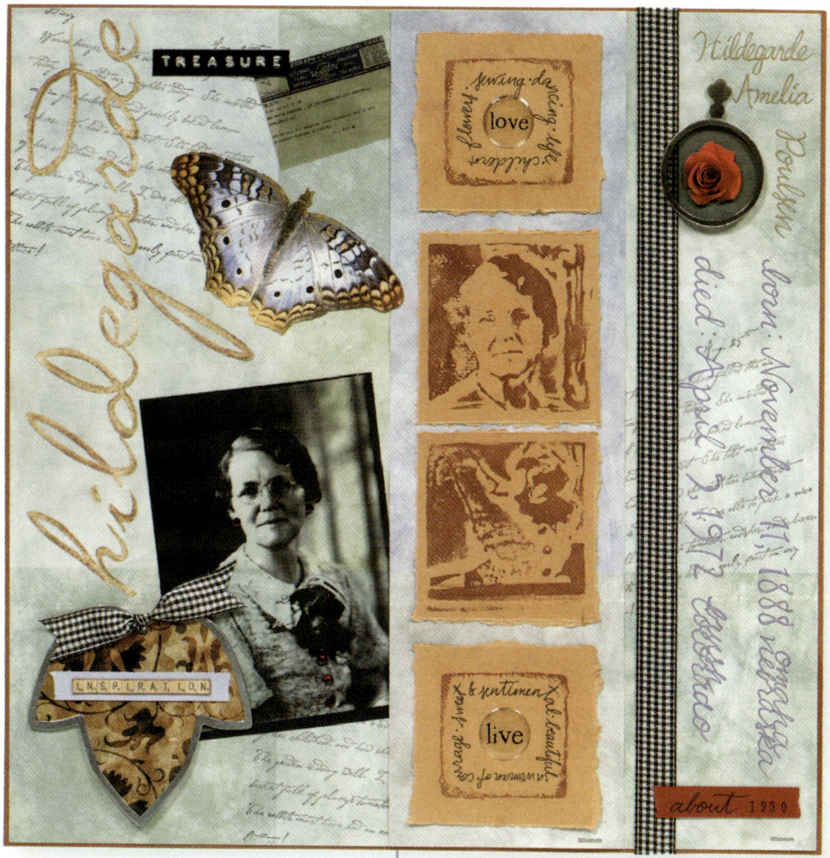

* Using a kit, Erikia made rubber stamps of this image of her grandmother and used them to embellish the page. She stamped the images as well as a square frame onto burnt orange card stock with embossing ink and then added metallic pigment powder. She used stickers to spell out her title and included handwritten journaling in a similar script written with a dip pen and ink with a metallic sheen.

Sources: Patterned paper, stickers, and metal-rim leaf tag by Sharon Soneff for Creative Imaginations. Rubber stamp (script background) by Love to Stamp. Rubber stamp kit by Artisan's Choice. Embossing ink by Ranger Industries. Pigment powder is Perfect Pearls by Ranger Industries. Calligraphy ink is Dr. Ph. Martins by Salis International. Label maker by Dymo. Collage materials by ArtChix Studio (telegraph and letter tiles) and Limited Edition Rubber Stamps (optical lens). Cutouts (butterfly and rose) by Paperhouse Productions. Rhinestones by JewelCraft. Ribbon by Offray. Design by Erikia Ghumm.

Custom rubber stamps. Turning your photographs into rubber stamps is a great way to transfer images. You can make them yourself using a kit by Artisan's Choice or have a custom rubber stamp company make one. This technique involves more work up front, but once you've had your stamp made, you can use it again and again. Because finding a company to make a custom photographic rubber stamp can be difficult, I like to make my own. You can purchase the Artisan's Choice kit online at www.artisanschoice.com. My favorite way to use photographic stamps is with specialty inks, embossing powders, and pigment powders.

Everything you need to make the stamps will come in the kit, including complete directions, but here's a quick recap of the process. Turn a digital image of your photograph into line art using photo-editing software. If you

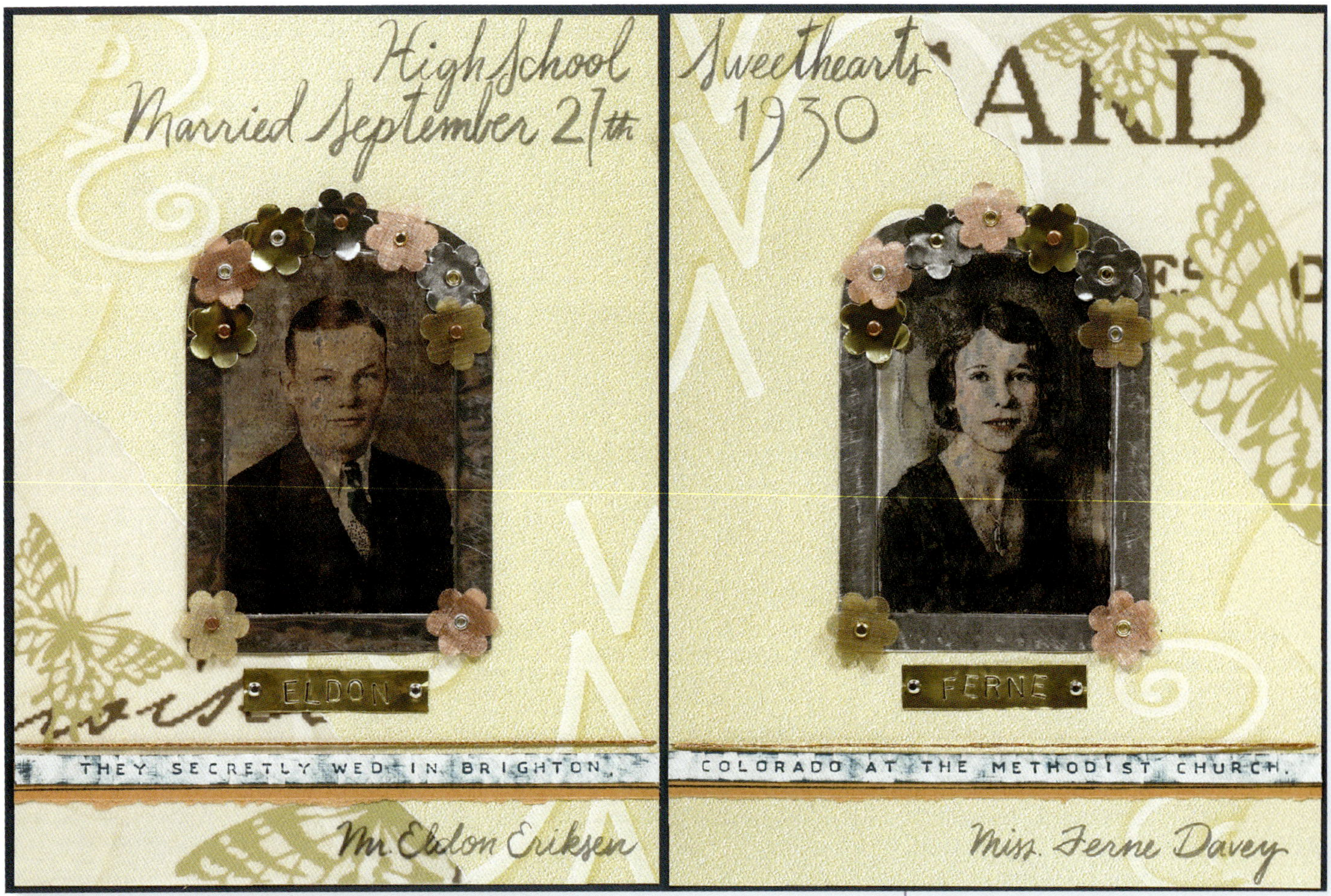

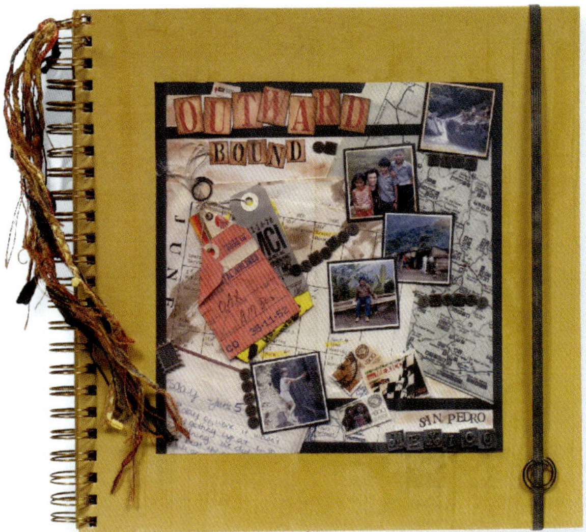

★ Erikia transferred these old images of her grandparents to shaped embossing foil using Lazertran. After transferring the images, she punched additional shapes from foil and mesh and attached them to the frames with eyelets and minibrads. She made the metal nameplates by imprinting strips of foil with steel letter stamps, rubbing the stamped pieces with metallic rub-ons to make the letters stand out.

Sources: Patterned paper by Club Scrap. Printed vellum by NRN Designs. Flower punch by Emagination Crafts. Metal stamps by Young Bros. Stamp Works Inc. Transfer medium by Lazertran. Label maker (turquoise strip at bottom) by Dymo. Fibers by Inkadinkado. Embossing foil and metal mesh by American Art and Clay Co. Eyelets by JewelCraft. Minibrads by Magic Scraps. Design by Erikia Ghumm.

★ For this album cover, Anita Matejka created a traditional scrapbook page that was meant to be a title page. She scanned the completed layout at 300 dpi, resized it in her image-editing program to fit an 8½x11-inch sheet of paper, and printed it onto ink-jet-safe Lazertran paper. After applying the image to the album, she gave the entire cover a coat of semigloss varnish to seal it.

Sources: Rubber stamps (alphabet) by PSX. Metal letters by Making Memories. Faux-metal letters ("Mexico") by Creative Imaginations. Metal postage stamp shape, postage stamp letters, and walnut ink by FoofaLa. Transfer medium by Lazertran. Glossy photo paper by Epson. Design by Anita Matejka.

don't have access to image-editing software, you can use a photocopier to get a suitable image. Enlarge the image as much as possible, copy it on a high-contrast setting, and then copy the copy to get an even higher-contrast image. Repeat as necessary, using a black felt-tip pen to touch up any voids left by the copier, and copy again, reducing the image to the original size.

Make a transparency copy of the image using a computer printer or a photocopier. Trim the transparency image to fit into the exposure tray that comes in the kit. Set up the included black light and place the transparency into the tray, adhering it with a dab of Casting Goop. Expose the tray to the black light to set the transparency. Now you can make the mold. This involves applying a thin layer of Casting Goop to the inside of the mold, exposing it to the black light, blotting up the uncured Casting Goop, and repeating these steps to build up the image. Once the mold is finished, mix up the Rubber Goop and pour it into the mold, allowing it to cure before removing. Trim the excess rubber from the image and mount it using the wood block included in the kit or an acrylic mounting system.

Lazertran. I think Lazertran is one of the most incredible products you can use to create image transfers. It's a water-slide transfer paper that's very versatile and can be applied to almost any type of surface, allowing you to produce a wide variety of looks, depending on which surface you decide to transfer the image to.

Experiment with transferring it to materials such as metal, watercolor paper, fabric, and wood. It can be purchased online at www.lazertran.com or at fine art stores.

Because Lazertran has so many uses, I would recommend reading the full package instructions before you begin. Photocopy the image you're working with in reverse directly onto a sheet of Lazertran. Use a high-end copy machine with a drum roller and be sure it does not use heat above 180° F to reproduce the image.

Choose the material you want to transfer an image to. Porous surfaces such as fabric, wood, and paper will need to be primed with gel medium and allowed to dry before the transfer is applied.

Cut or tear the image from the full sheet and place the image in a shallow tub of water to release the image from the backing sheet. Gently remove the image from the water and place it on your surface. Before placing the image onto your project, you may need to apply another coat of the gel medium to use as an adhesive. Once it's in place, remove all the air bubbles, smooth it down with a brayer or squeegee, and allow it to dry.

Nonporous surfaces need no priming. Just cut or tear the image from the Lazertran page and place it in a shallow tub of water to release the image from the backing sheet. This will also activate the adhesive on the back of the image, and it should be sufficient enough to adhere it to your project. Remove the air bubbles, smooth it with a brayer or squeegee, and allow it to dry. If desired, you can further enhance the image with acrylic paints.

Now that you've been exposed to the world of image transfers, I hope you'll give the different techniques a try. I think you'll find that you can push your photographs to a place you never thought possible and truly let your creativity run wild.

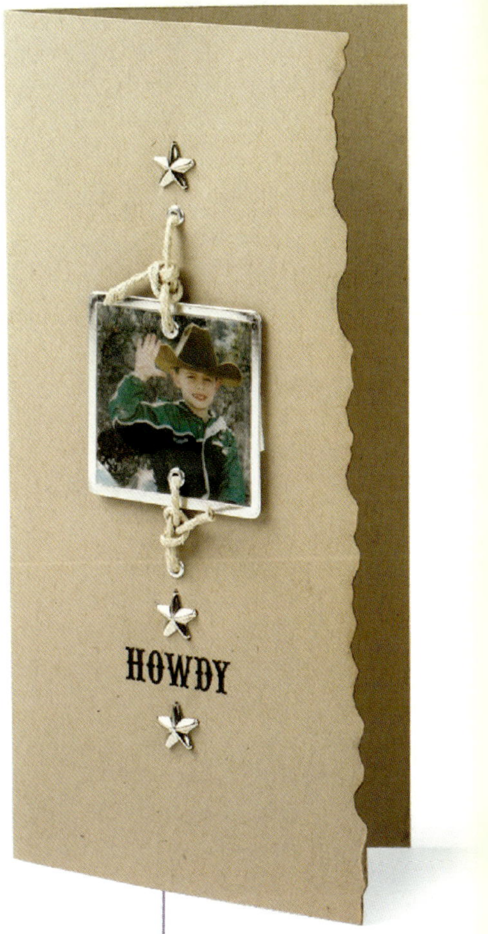

★ Polly Maly transferred a photo of her son Cole to a vellum metal-rim tag using the packing tape transfer method. She used vellum adhesive to attach the image to the tag and attached the tag to the card with jute and eyelets.

Sources: Computer font is URW Wood Type by URW++. Metal-rim tag by Making Memories. Star studs by Scrapworks. Eyelets by Doodlebug Design. Design by Polly Maly.

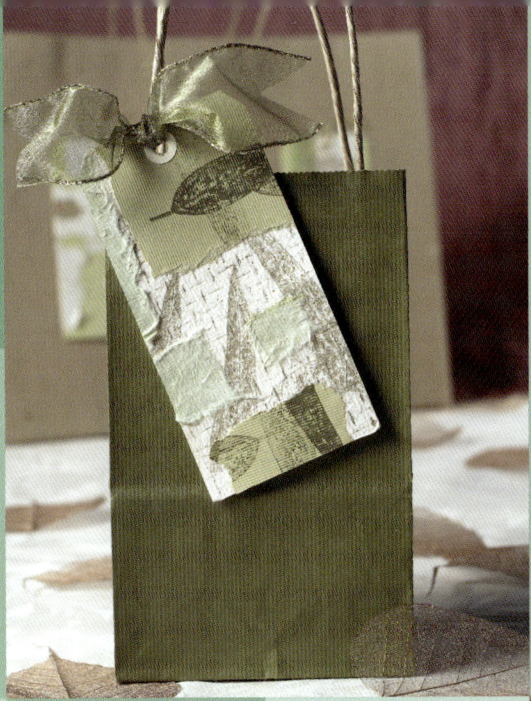

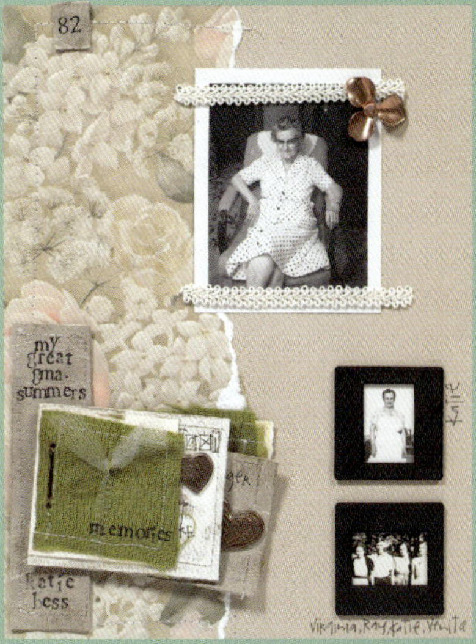

82
my great gma summers
memories

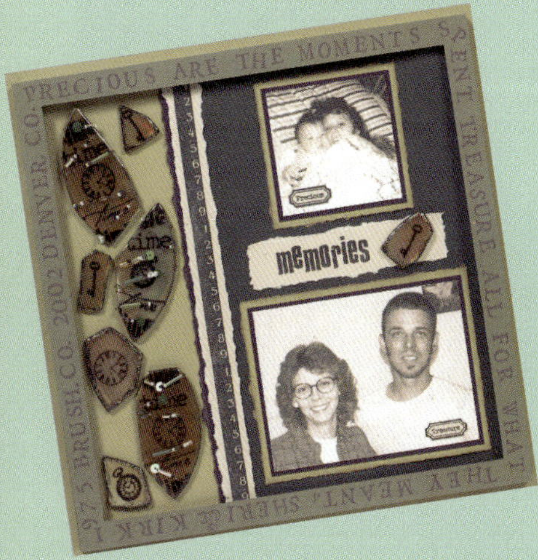

PRECIOUS ARE THE MOMENTS SPENT
TREASURE ALL FOR WHAT THEY MEANT
memories

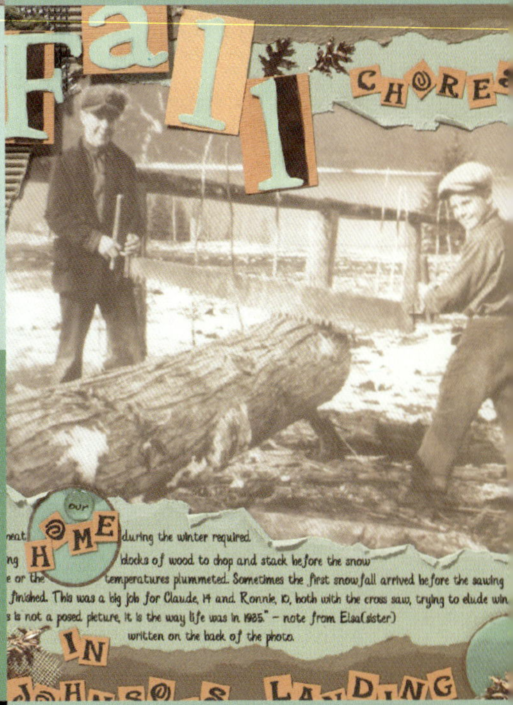

Fall
CHORES
our HOME
during the winter required
blocks of wood to chop and stack before the snow
temperatures plummeted. Sometimes the first snowfall arrived before the sawing
finished. This was a big job for Claude, 14 and Ronnie, 10, both with the cross saw, trying to elude win
is not a posed picture, it is the way life was in 1935." – note from Elsa(sister)
written on the back of the photo.
IN
LANDING

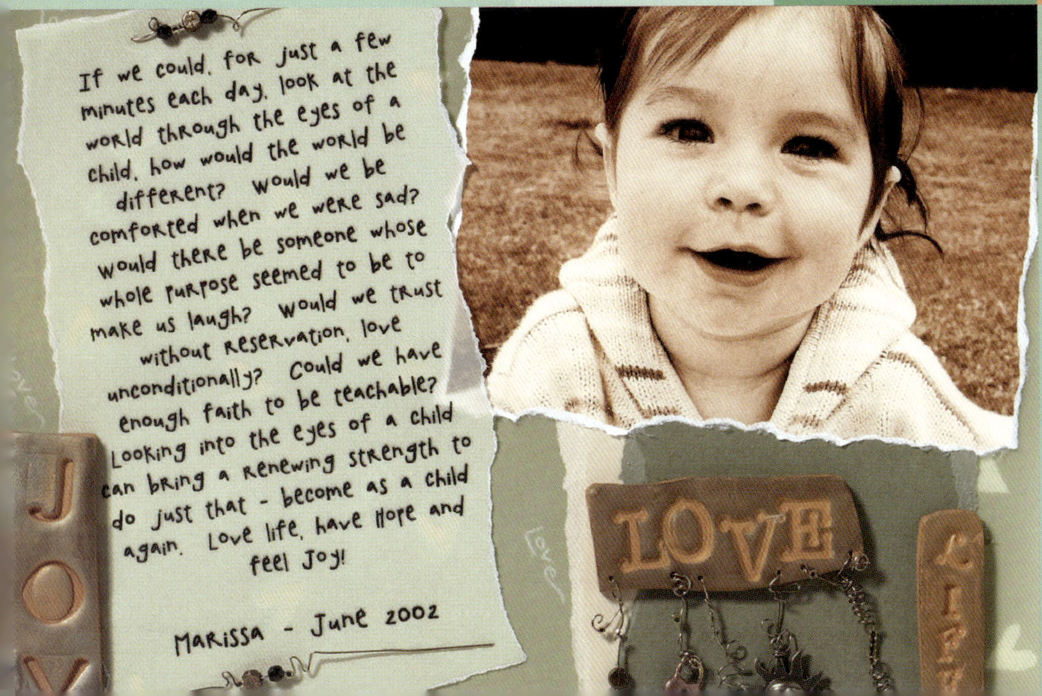

If we could, for just a few minutes each day, look at the world through the eyes of a child, how would the world be different? Would we be comforted when we were sad? Would there be someone whose whole purpose seemed to be to make us laugh? Would we trust without reservation, love unconditionally? Could we have enough faith to be teachable? Looking into the eyes of a child can bring a renewing strength to do just that - become as a child again. Love life, have Hope and feel Joy!
Marissa - June 2002
LOVE
JOY

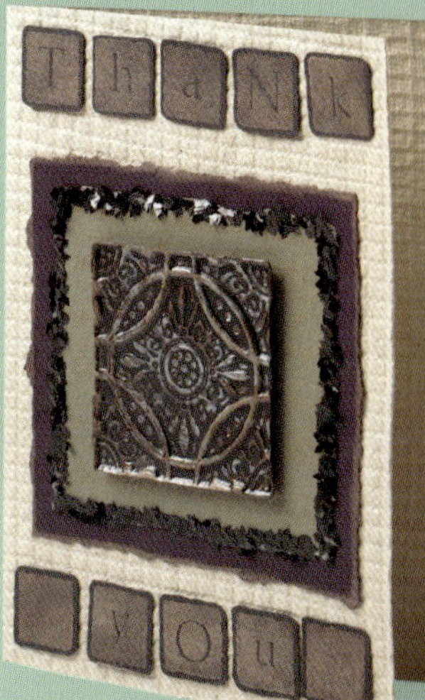

Thank
you

great ideas gallery

Scrapbook pages are as personal as the choice of materials, as unique as the subjects in the photos, and as individual as the crafters who make them. That's why it's such fun to share designs with scrapping friends. Use these great ideas in your own albums, or let the compositions and concepts inspire you to a new level of paper artistry.

tag it!

Enjoy paper tags with a **RENEWED FOCUS,** and use them as artistic embellishments and to journal your scrapbooking **ADVENTURES.**

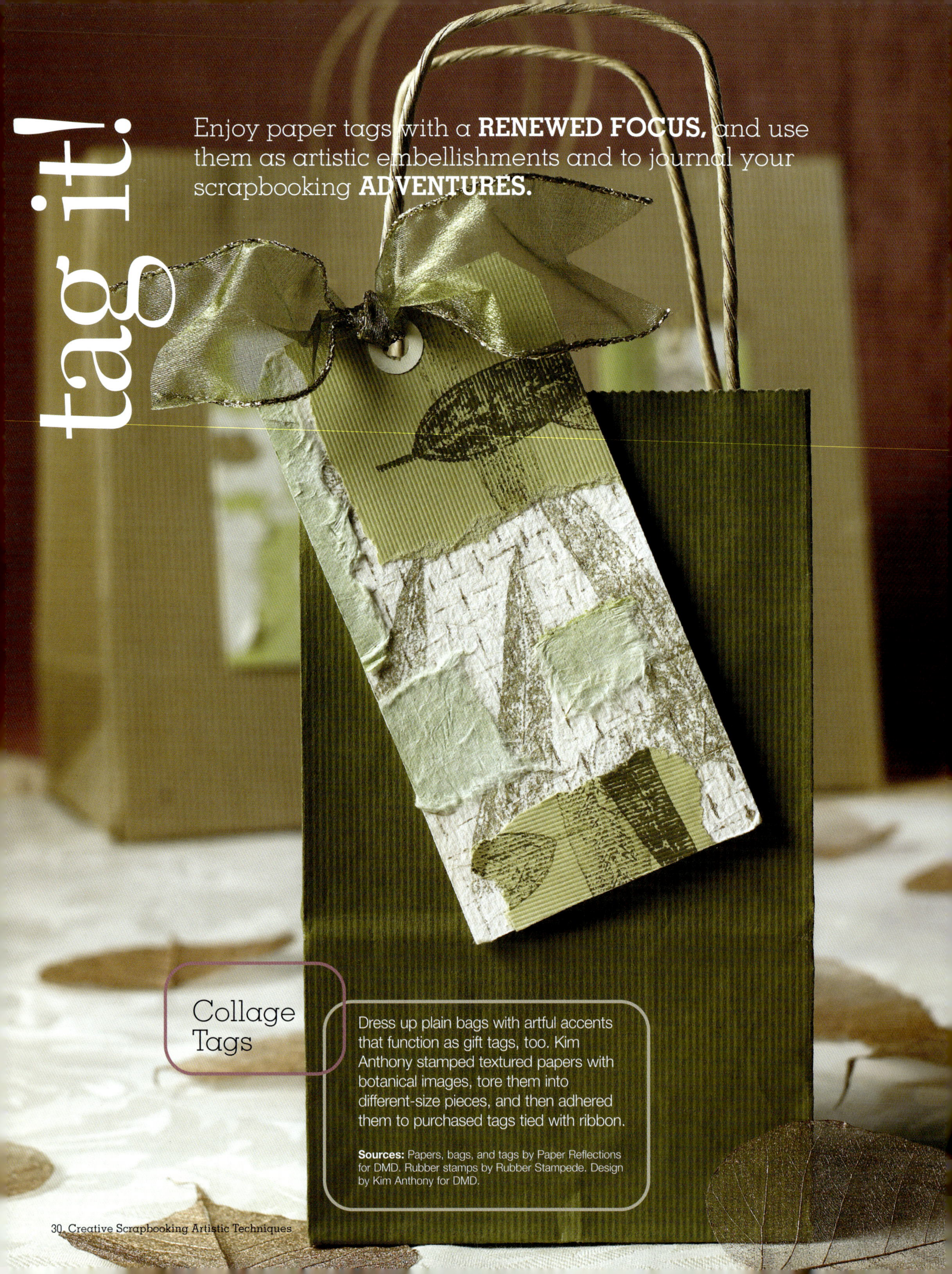

Collage Tags

Dress up plain bags with artful accents that function as gift tags, too. Kim Anthony stamped textured papers with botanical images, tore them into different-size pieces, and then adhered them to purchased tags tied with ribbon.

Sources: Papers, bags, and tags by Paper Reflections for DMD. Rubber stamps by Rubber Stampede. Design by Kim Anthony for DMD.

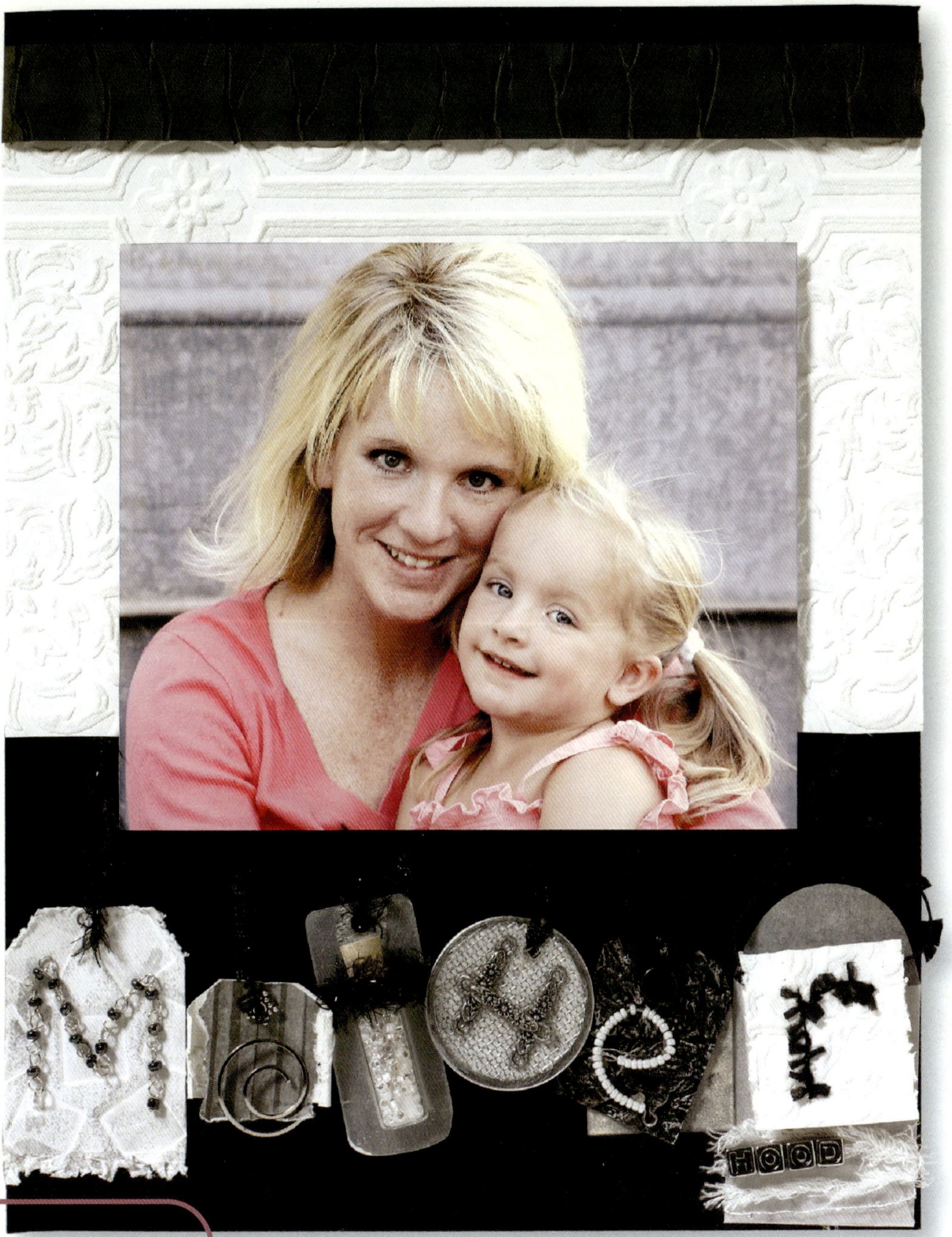

Motherhood

The tag collages of British artist Sarah Lugg totally captivate Danelle Johnson. "When I first saw Lugg's work, it stopped me," Danelle says. "All I could do is study it and enjoy it." She started to save copies of Lugg's art on her computer, knowing that one day she wanted to create something with a similar vision. She did it here, using unique materials and backgrounds for each of the tagged letters on her layout.

Sources: Patterned paper by Mustard Moon. Decorative paper by Solum World Papers. Metal tag by Magic Scraps. Fibers by Adornaments for K1C2. Beads by Shipwreck Beads. Glass bottle from Twopeasinabucket.com. Metal letter beads by Crafts Etc!. Design by Danelle Johnson.

Proud to Be American

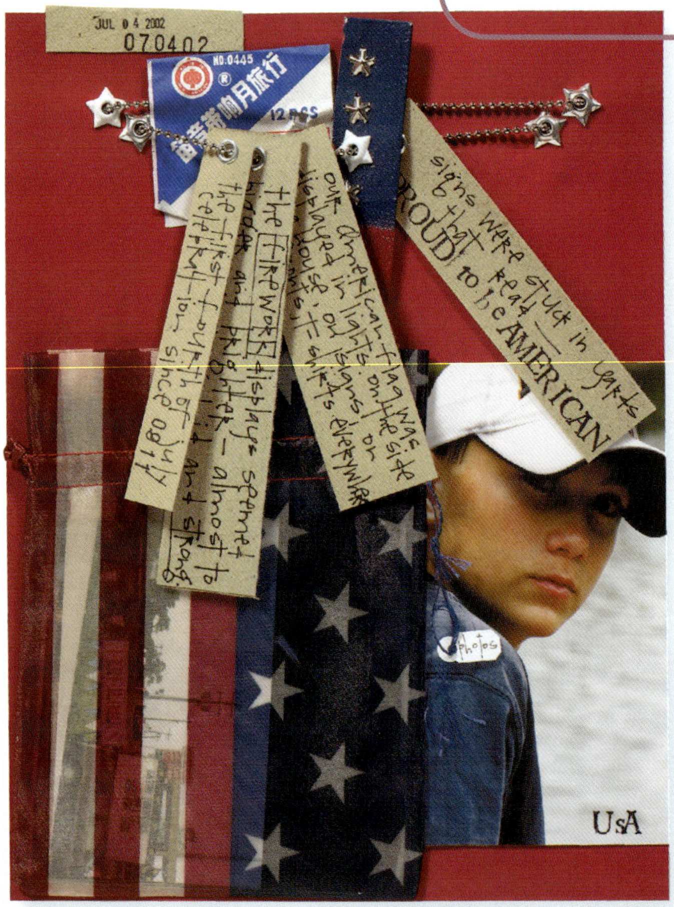

The first Fourth of July after the tragedies of September 11, 2001, was especially meaningful for many Americans, including the McAtee family. To commemorate their feelings and displays of patriotism, Stephanie McAtee created this stars-and-stripes layout. Steph knew she wanted to include a lot of elements, so to keep the layout from becoming overly cluttered, she focused on one photograph and slipped the extra photos inside a fabric flag bag. To balance these two large images at the bottom of her page, Steph added a string of journaling tags across the top, using strips of brown card stock, eyelets, and a beaded chain. She also inked and embossed one strip to resemble a miniflag and attached it with star brads and eyelets. A wrapper from a fireworks package gives the page extra lift.

Sources: Alphabet stamps by PSX. Star eyelets by The Stamp Doctor. Fabric flag bag by Memory Lane. Design by Stephanie McAtee.

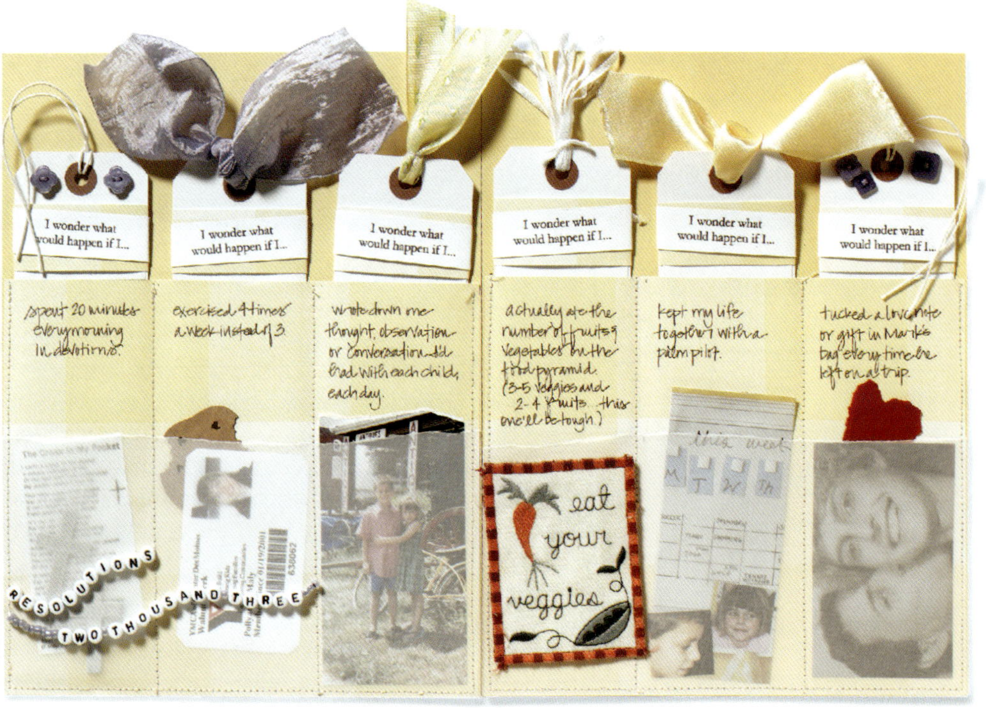

Will's World

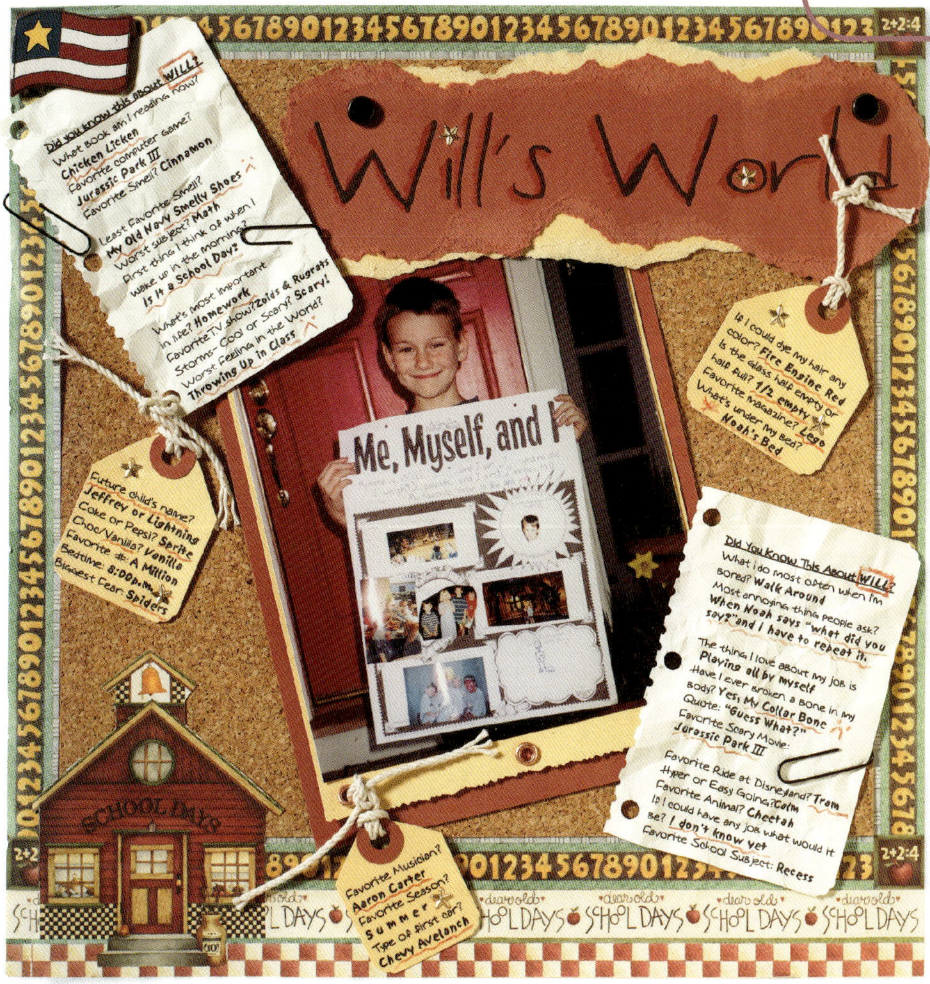

Susan Badgett used a question-and-answer format for the journaling on this layout about her son Will and the poster he did for school. She interviewed him about all sorts of things, asking about his fears, his habits, and his least favorite smell! Then she printed the interview on manila and white papers, cutting the journaling to look like tags and notebook papers.

Sources: Patterned paper by Debbie Mumm for Creative Imaginations. Cork paper by Magenta. Computer fonts are Sand (answers) by Apple Computer Inc. and Herbert (questions) downloaded off the Internet. Black brads by Officemate International. Wooden flag by Provo Craft. Design by Susan Badgett.

What Would Happen If I ...

Polly Maly has always found herself drawn to anything with pockets—so she knew that a pocket design for her resolutions pages would be ideal for inserting tags that represent her year-long goals. She also thought it would be a great idea to keep her resolutions in "check" by placing progress updates throughout the year in corresponding pockets. To make the tiered-pockets design, Polly cut and layered two shades of gold card stock along with a torn piece of vellum. Using her sewing machine, she stitched four vertical lines, creating three pockets on each page. She added buttons, ribbon hangers, and labels to luggage tags that fit into the top row of pockets. In the vellum pockets, she tucked photographs and photocopies of memorabilia. Alphabet beads strung onto a wire spell out the title and year.

Sources: Patterned paper by Anna Griffin. Chocolate chip cookie die cut by Deluxe Cuts. Buttons by LaMode. Ribbon by Offray. Alphabet beads by Westrim Crafts. Lavender beads by Crafts Etc!. White luggage tags by Heirlooms by Design. Fibers by On the Surface. Design by Polly Maly.

a play of textures

Although not **TRADITIONALLY** used in paper crafting, products like polymer clay, metal, and even plastic CDs can give your designs just the **OOMPH** you've been looking for.

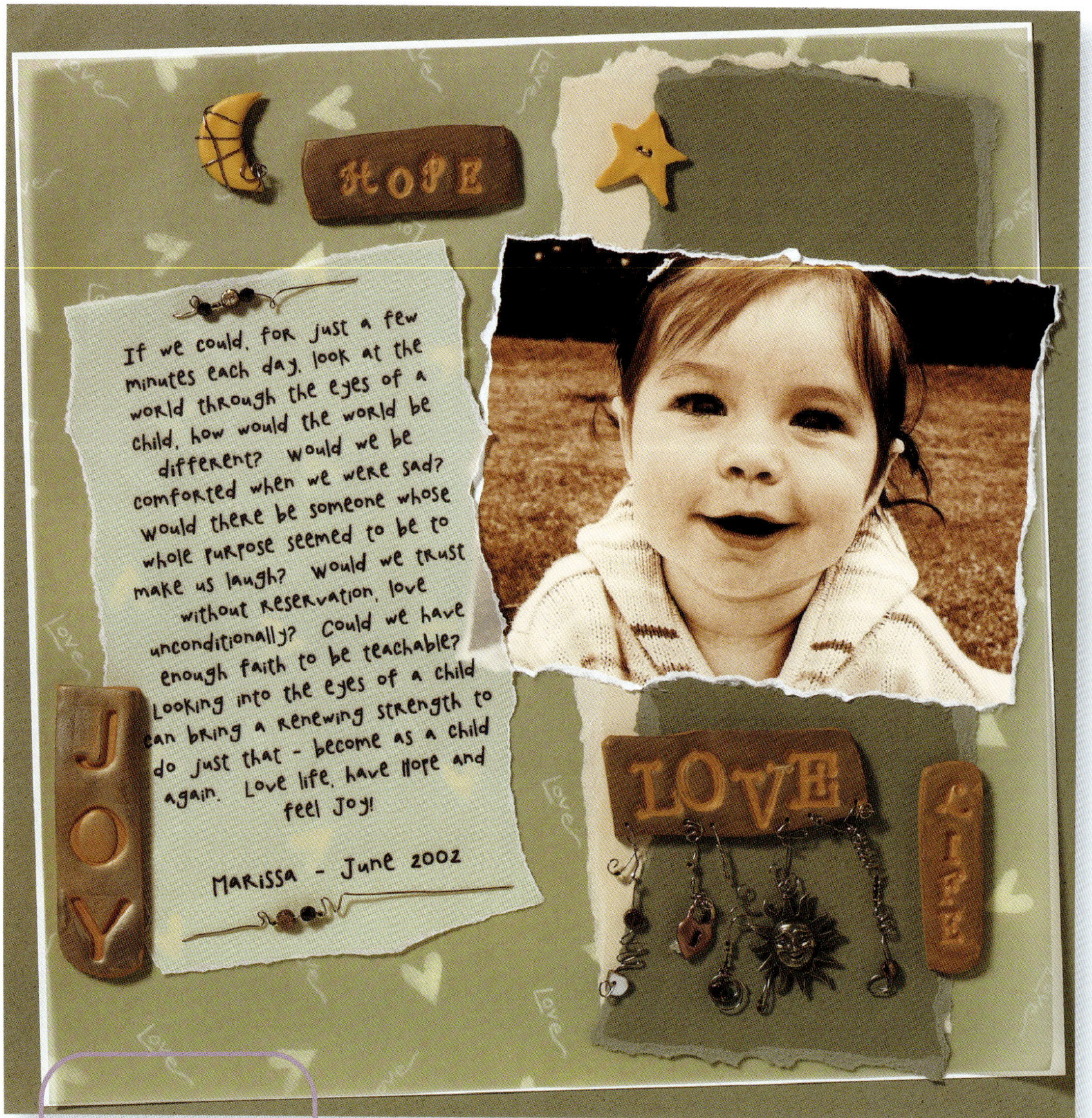

Hope, Joy, Love, Life

Helen Naylor used rubber stamps to impress words in flattened lengths of polymer clay for this layout. She poked holes along the bottom edge of the "Love" piece and then inserted wire dressed up with beads and charms after the pieces were baked. She gave the finished pieces shine with metallic rub-ons.

Sources: Polymer clay by Sculpey. Patterned vellum by Sweetwater. Computer font (journaling) is Chicken Shack by Melissa Baxter for Twopeasinabucket.com. Rubber stamps by Club Scrap (Joy), Susan Branch (Hope and Life), and Printworks (Life). Design by Helen Naylor.

Thank-You Card

For the intricate accent on the front of this card, Erikia Ghumm primed her rubber stamp with a generous amount of pigment ink and then dipped the stamp in a Melting Pot filled with Ultra Thick Embossing Enamel (UTEE), being careful not to cover the foam or wood portion of the stamp with the hot liquid. After allowing the excess enamel to drip off, she turned the stamp over to allow the enamel to settle and cool. Once it was cool to the touch, she freed the piece from the stamp and adhered it to the card with Glue Dots.

Sources: Card by Hero Arts. Melting Pot, Ultra Thick Embossing Enamel, and Diamondz by Suze Weinberg for Ranger Industries. Rubber stamps by Hero Arts (alphabet) and Magenta (decorative image). Design by Erikia Ghumm.

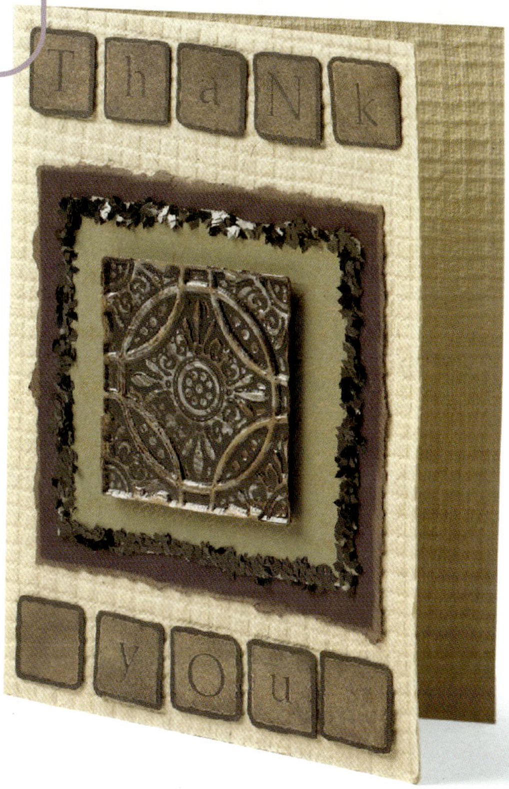

Memories

Don't throw away the CDs you get in the mail! Instead, use them to create beautiful works of art. Here Erikia Ghumm stamped directly on the holographic side of a CD with permanent dye ink. She cut the CD into pieces with a pair of sharp scissors, warming the CD with a heat tool first to make it more pliable. Using tweezers, Erikia dipped the stamped CD pieces in the Melting Pot filled with Ultra Thick Embossing Enamel (UTEE). She wiped the back off with the Kool Toolz spatula to create a smooth surface for adhering. To even out the UTEE on the CD and to remove any marks left by the tweezers, she reheated the CD pieces with a heat tool. Erikia uses E-6000 or Wonder Tape to add CD pieces to layouts.

Sources: Rubber stamps by Limited Edition Rubber Stamps (key, pocket watch, clock face, ruler, "time, time, time," "memories," "precious," and "treasure") and Stamp Craft (alphabet used on frame). Ultra Thick Embossing Enamel, To Dye For Inks, Kool Toolz Spatula, and Melting Pot by Suze Weinberg for Ranger Industries. Glitter glue by Ranger Industries. Beads and sequins by JewelCraft. Design by Erikia Ghumm.

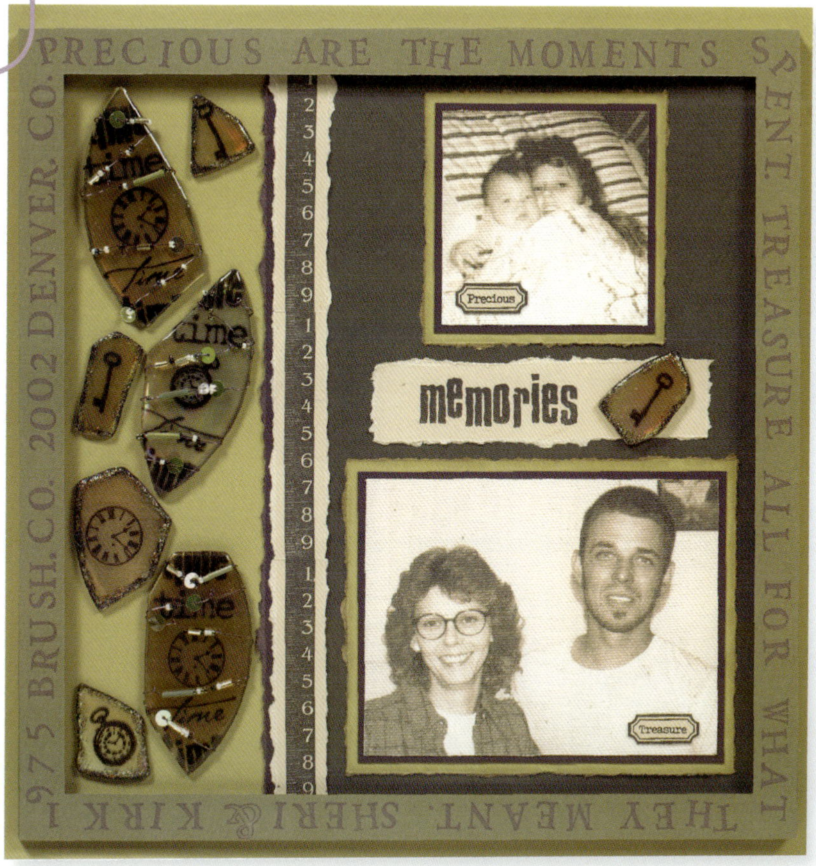

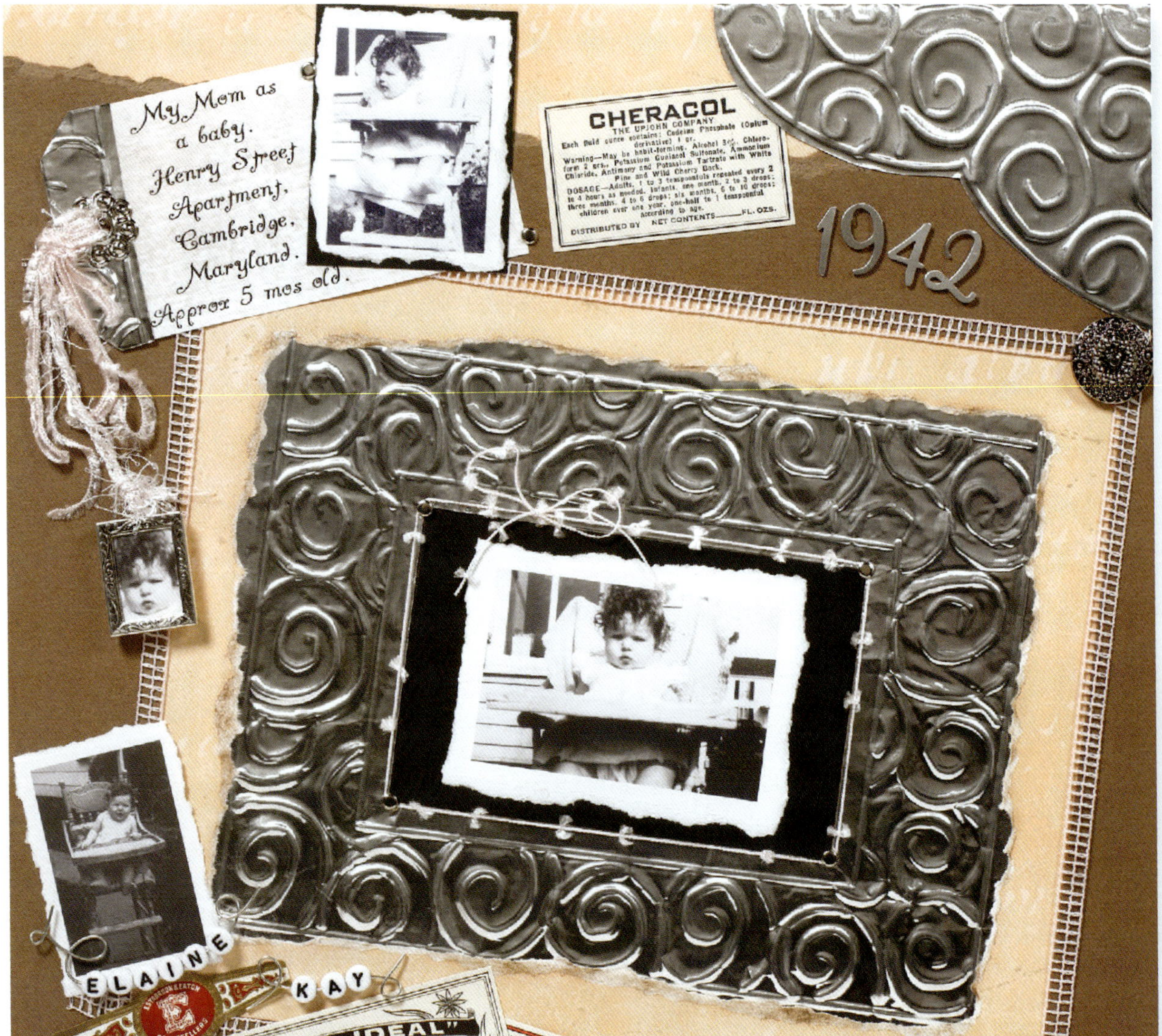

1942 Elaine Kay Price

Embossed crafting metal sets this page in the softest swirls. Kathleen Paneitz created the repetitive texture using an embossing stylus and a rubber-stamped image. She stamped the back of the metal with a frame stamp and then added length and width to the frame by stamping it again on the ends. She also stamped the image on the metal for the large corner embellishment. For the raised effect, Kathleen traced over the lines on both pieces with a stylus, creating a freehand curve for the corner piece.

Sources: Patterned paper by PSX. Computer font is A Yummy Apology downloaded off the Internet. Rubber stamp by All Night Media. ArtEmboss crafting metal by American Art Clay Co. Metal numbers by Making Memories. Extreme Eyelet and Shotz Tag by Creative Imaginations. Fibers by Adornaments for EK Success. Alphabet beads by Crafts Etc!. Silver minibrads by Scrap Art. Watch face and pharmacy labels by Artchix Studio. Frame charm by Impress Rubber Stamps. Design by Kathleen Paneitz.

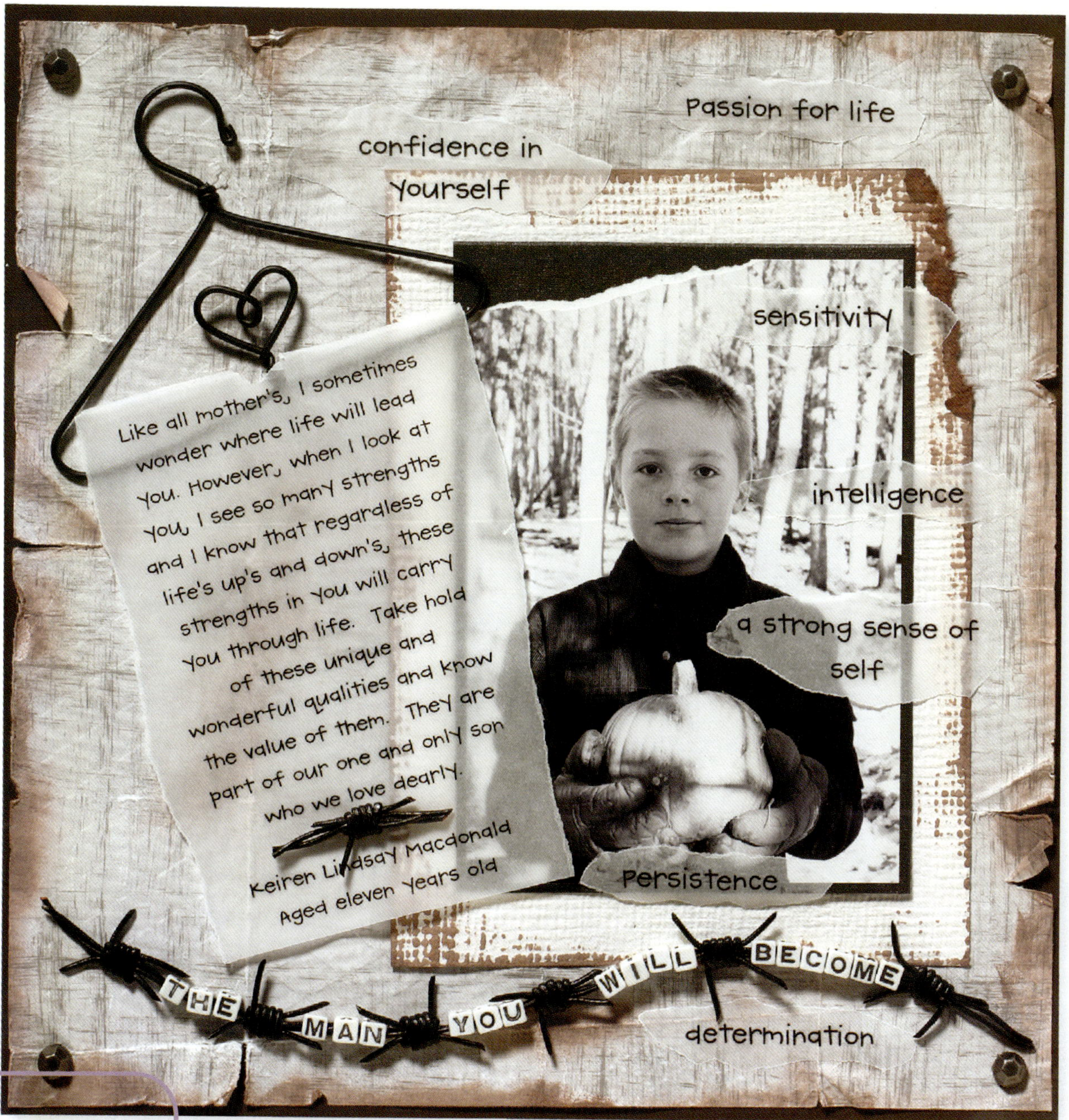

The Man You Will Become

When Colleen Macdonald sat down to create this page for her son, she had difficulty coming up with "masculine" scrapbooking supplies. So this layout required a lot of design initiative. Colleen liked the paper she found but felt it lacked character. She distressed it, folding it into smaller and smaller squares and lightly rubbing it with a metal scourer. The fake barbed wire was bought at a leather supply store. Colleen cut it so she could thread it with letter blocks. For more texture, she ripped a corner of her photo and photo mat, smudging both with a stamp pad, and then added corner studs and a wire hanger to hold the journaling block.

Sources: Patterned paper by Mustard Moon. Stamp ink by Colorbök for Clearsnap. Alphabet beads by The Beadery. Metal Studs by Beads & Plenty More. Design by Colleen Macdonald.

forever in my heart

Heritage pages let you share stories and **MEMORIES** of loved ones from your **FAMILY** tree with a new generation.

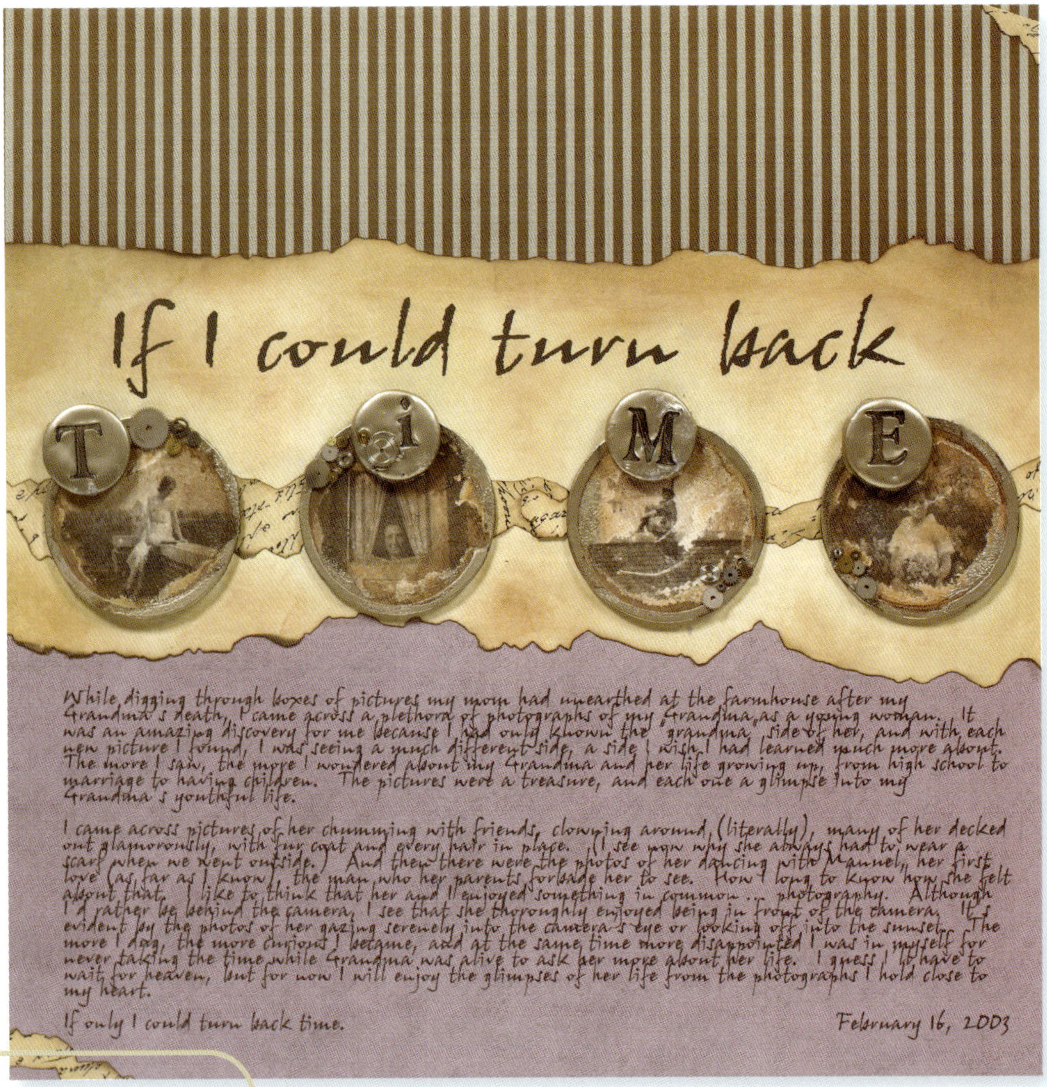

If I Could Turn Back Time

When Anita Matejka discovered these photos of her grandmother, she could record the images for her photo album, but sadly, not all the memories that belonged to them. For her photo tags, Anita combined image-transfer and embossing techniques. She used a gel medium to transfer the images to large tags, further aging the images by daubing ink and embossing powder around the edges. (For more on image transfers, see page 22.) To create letter discs, Anita inked wood pieces with pigment ink and dipped them in Ultra Thick Embossing Enamel (UTEE). She repeated the process, building up the enamel, and then added embossing powder, melting it with a heat gun. While the powder was still hot, she stamped the letters, revealing the pigment ink below.

Sources: Patterned paper by K&Company (stripes), Penny Black (text), and Karen Foster Design (tan). Rubber stamps by PSX. Computer font is John Handy downloaded off the Internet. Metal-rim tags by American Tag Co. Embossing enamel by Suze Weinberg. Embossing powder by PSX. Wood discs by Lara's Crafts. Design by Anita Matejka.

My Great-Grandma Summers

Stephanie McAtee made this layout in honor of her great-grandmother Katie Bess Summers. Although Steph was young when her great-grandmother passed away, she still felt close to her and created this page to preserve the memories she has. The highlight of this design is Steph's minibook of memories. Using fabrics, vellum, chipboard, and card stock, Steph made four pages for the book. The chipboard was crumpled, inked, and smoothed to give it an aged look and a texture similar to leather. Each page is embellished with charms, stitching, or stamping and has at least one of Steph's memories of her great-grandmother handwritten on it. The book is bound and attached to the page with copper wire.

Sources: Patterned paper by K&Company. Alphabet stamps by PSX. Slide mounts by Impress Rubber Stamps. Mesh ribbon by Magic Scraps. Copper embellishments by Anima Designs. Metallic rub-ons by Craf-T Products. Design by Stephanie McAtee.

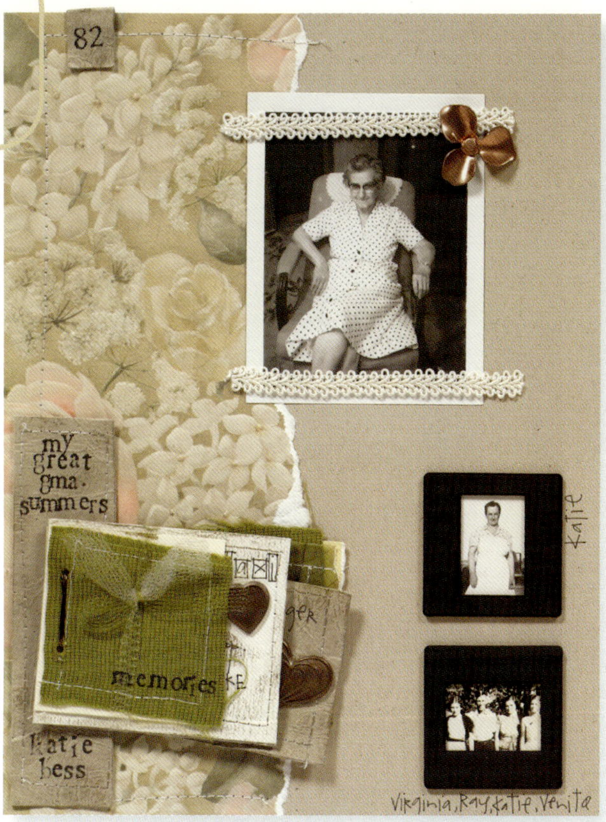

Travel Log–The DeSoto

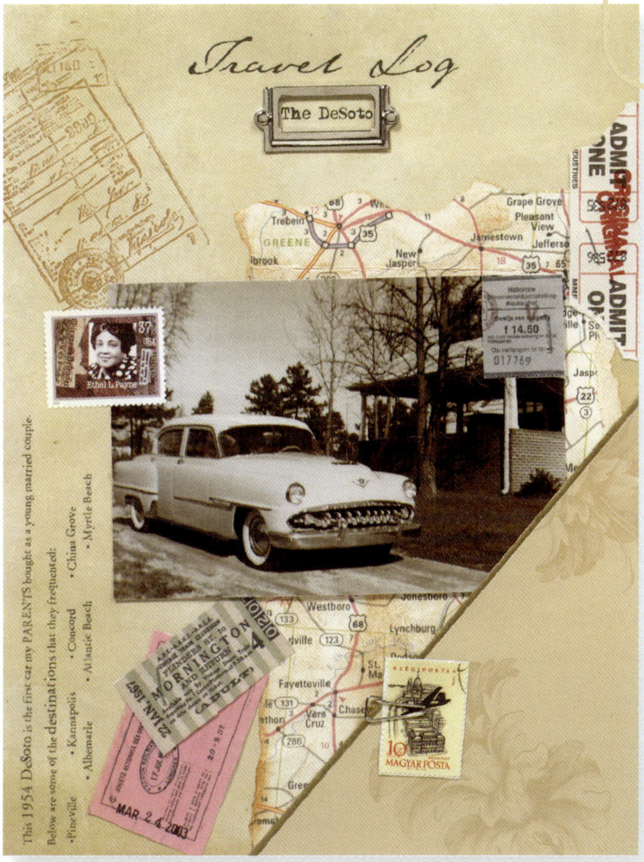

While helping her mother organize photographs, Faye Morrow Bell found this image of her parents' first car. Faye was eager to create a scrapbook page to capture some of the memories of the "new" car, and after interviewing her mother about the DeSoto, she got to work. Faye started the page by printing her journaling and titles directly onto the background paper. Next, she aged a section of torn map-patterned paper by adding ink to it, crumpling it, and smoothing it out. Postage stamps, ticket stubs, and other tidbits help complete the collage look of the layout.

Sources: Patterned paper by Paper Pizazz for Hot Off the Press (map), Karen Foster Design (background), and Frances Meyer (floral). Computer fonts are Garamouche (journaling) by P22 and Texas Hero (title) and Mom's Typewriter ("The DeSoto") downloaded off the Internet. Rubber stamps by Stampers Anonymous (passport page) and Office Depot (date). Bookplate by Twopeasinabucket.com. Postage stamps by Stampa Rosa. Brads by American Fastener. Ephemera by Limited Edition Rubber Stamps. Design by Faye Morrow Bell.

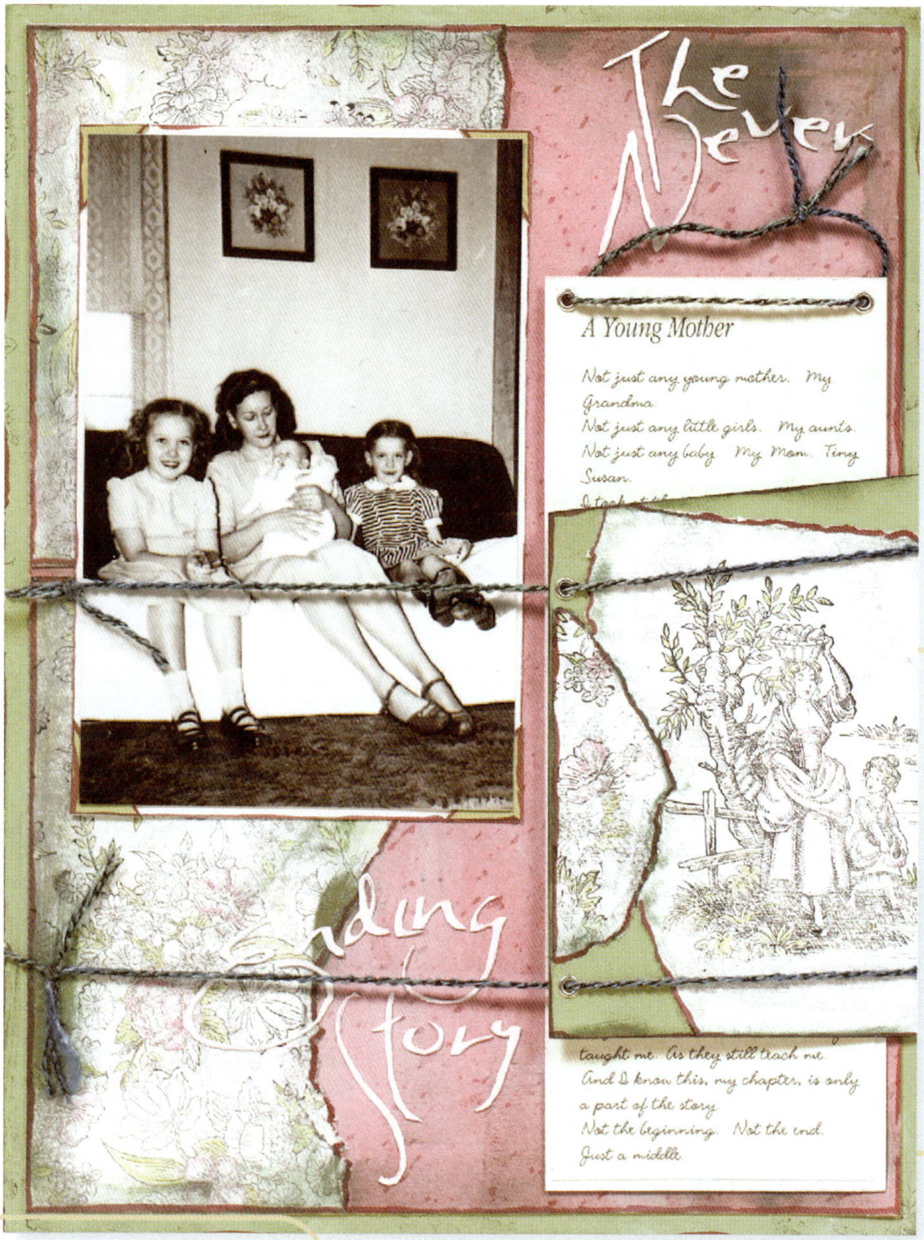

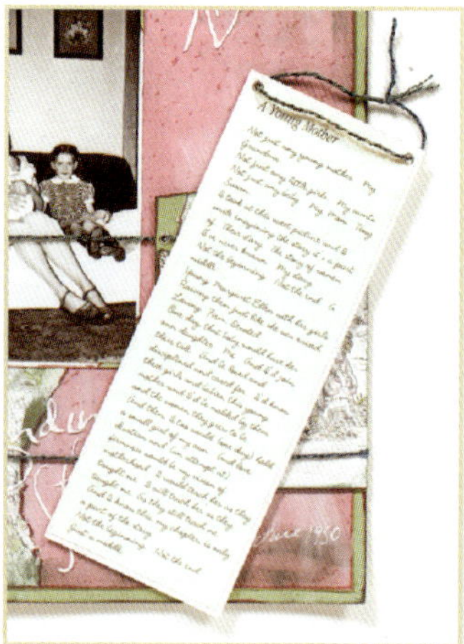

The Never-Ending Story

Nicole Gartland always thinks of fairy tales when she sees this photo of her grandmother surrounded by her three daughters. (The infant in the photo is Nicole's mother.) To stress the timeless theme of her journaling, Nicole chose stamps that looked classical, as if they could have been illustrations from an old book. To create the flap on the right side of the page, Nicole started with a 12-inch square of green card stock and then measured out an 8½×11-inch section on the left side of the square. She drew the flap on the right side as she wanted it, cut away the excess card stock, and then folded the flap in toward the page. The journaling block slips into the fold. Nicole enhanced the stamped image with colored pencils and added colorful fibers to keep the flap closed.

Sources: Patterned paper by The Paper Loft. Computer fonts are Scrap Script (journaling) by Inspire Graphics, Gingersnap (title) by Twopeasinabucket.com, and BD Oxford ("A Young Mother") downloaded off the Internet. Rubber stamps by All Night Media. Eyelets by Making Memories. Fibers by Rubba Dub Dub. Design by Nicole Gartland.

Grammy Boles

Susan Badgett's grandmother introduced her to scrapbooking when she was just a girl, making her an ABC album from recycled cards and magazine pages for her fifth birthday. When she found this photo of her grandmother and herself looking through one of her scrapbooks, Susan knew she had to create a special layout honoring her scrapbooking origins. "Besides being a scrapbooker, Grammy loved to do crossword puzzles and play Scrabble," Susan says. So Susan used paper Scrabble tiles to spell out the answers to a personal history crossword puzzle. "When I told Mom I was doing this layout, she dug out this flapper photo of Grammy in the 1920s as well as a 1950s photo of the two of them together," Susan says. "By showing three generations, I feel it really conveys the 'circle of scrapbook life' theme I was going for."

Sources: Computer font is Courier by Adobe. Printed tags are Fresh Cuts tags by Rebecca Sower for EK Success. Leaf and twig accents are Flash Frames and Accents by Forget Me Not Designs. Stickers are Sonnets by Sharon Soneff for Creative Imaginations. Scrabble tiles by Somerset Studio. Design by Susan Badgett.

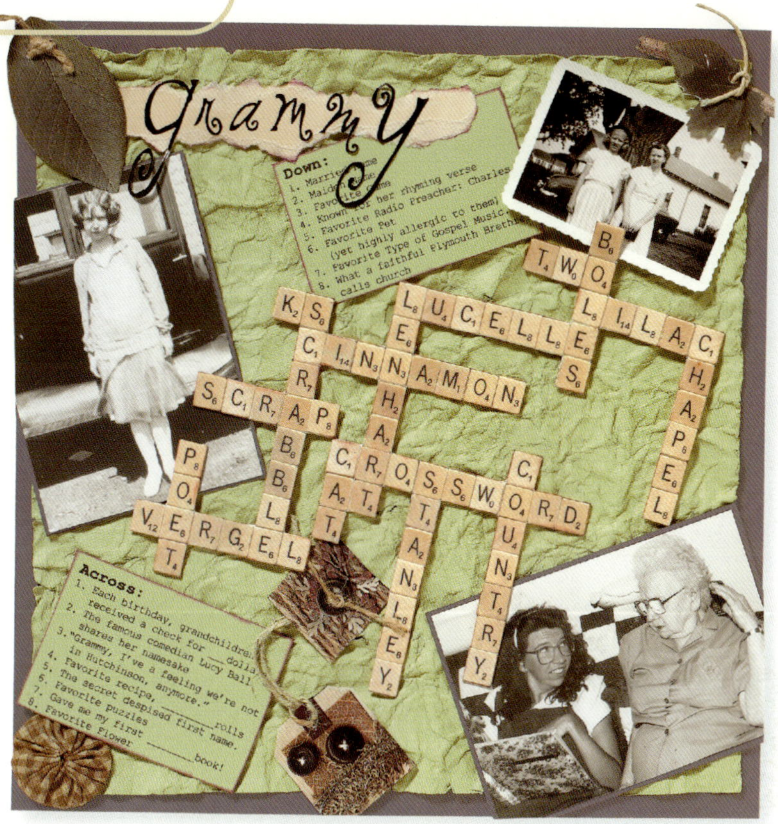

Fall Chores

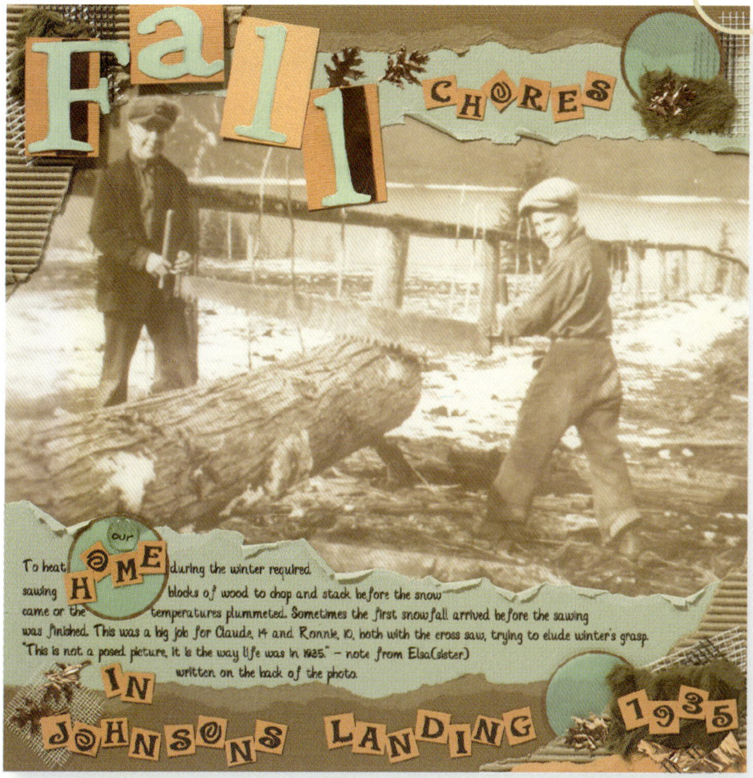

Sharon Whitehead designed this layout around an old photo of her father and uncle hard at work. The picture was taken in 1935, and the work at hand was sawing and stacking enough wood for cooking and heating their home through the winter. Sharon is grateful to have these family photos, especially since they show a part of the young boys' everyday life. Sharon first enlarged the photo so that it could become part of the background. To make the page look like it was peeled away, exposing the photo beneath, she layered card stock with torn edges on top of the photo. Orange and green colors amid textures of copper foil, mesh, and corrugated paper accent the sepia-toned photo and strengthen the fall theme.

Sources: Card stock by Bazzill Basics Paper. Corrugated paper by Timports. Handmade paper by Victoria Art Supply. Computer fonts are Garamouche (title) by P22 and PC Becca Brush (journaling) by Provo Craft. Copper foil by Scrap Metal. Plastic mesh by Magic Mesh. Pebble by Making Memories. Punches by Marvy Uchida (circle) and Emagination Crafts (leaf). Design by Sharon Whitehead.

the beauty around us

The idea for a collage page and the **INSPIRATION** for all kinds of **TACTILE** elements may be right outside your door!

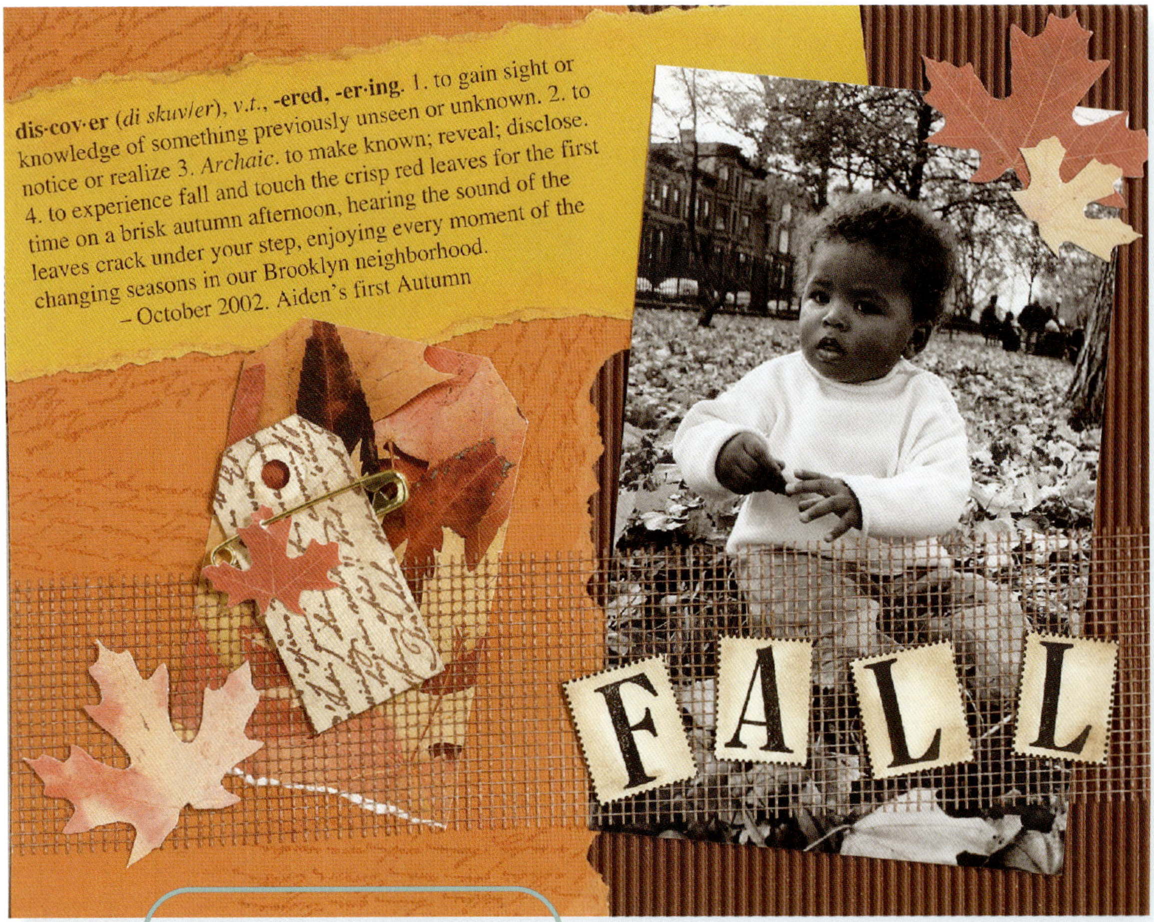

Discovering Fall

Nia Reddy wanted this layout about her son's first fall to focus on discovery, so she used the dictionary definition of "discover" as part of her journaling. To personalize the meaning, Nia added the last of the numbered definitions to describe the sights and sounds of the season. Because she chose a black-and-white photo, Nia wanted to give the page additional punch by using vibrant card stocks and papers with rich textures. She picked all her colors based on the purchased leaf and leaf tag die cuts and used corrugated cardboard, woven mesh, and faux-postage-stamp letters.

Sources: Computer font is Times New Roman by Agfa-Monotype. Leaves and leaf tag by Forget Me Not Designs. Script stamp by Stampa Rosa. Plastic mesh by Magic Mesh. Postage stamp alphabet by FoofaLa. Small tag by 7Gypsies. Design by Nia Reddy.

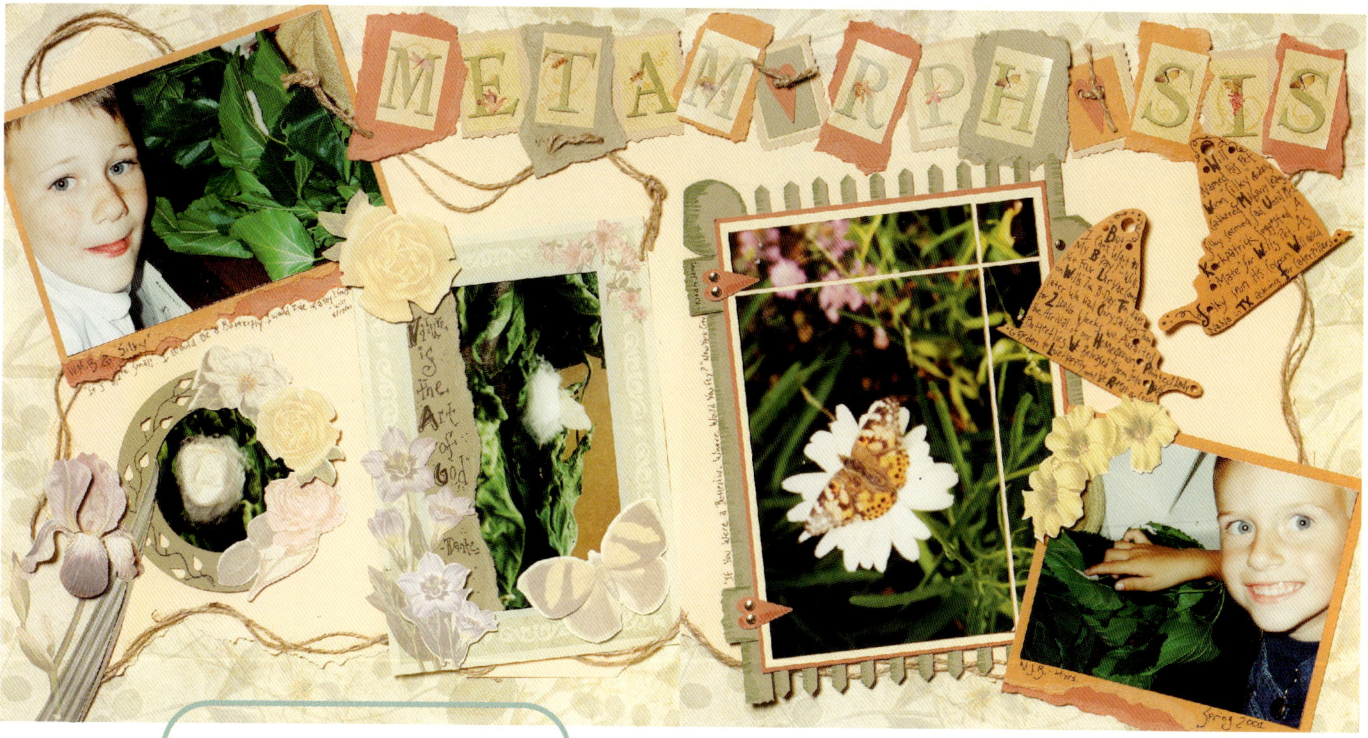

Metamorphosis

When Susan Badgett and her sons Will and Noah began raising their own Painted Lady butterflies, they decided it would be fun to capture the metamorphosis on film. They watched over a period of weeks as the creatures transformed from wiggly caterpillars to beautiful butterflies. Susan layered floral die cuts, sticker letters, and torn paper to embellish the photo-documentary, giving the butterflies dimension by sandwiching adhesive foam between the wings. Never one to fear the unusual, Susan added an empty cocoon that once housed one of their "pets."

Sources: Patterned paper by K&Company. Punches by Emagination Crafts (heart), McGill, Inc. (teardrop), and Family Treasures (large circle). Die cuts by K&Company (flowers and frames) and Accu-Cut Systems (butterflies). Alphabet stickers by K&Company. The picket fence is Susan's design (pattern on page 47). Design by Susan Badgett.

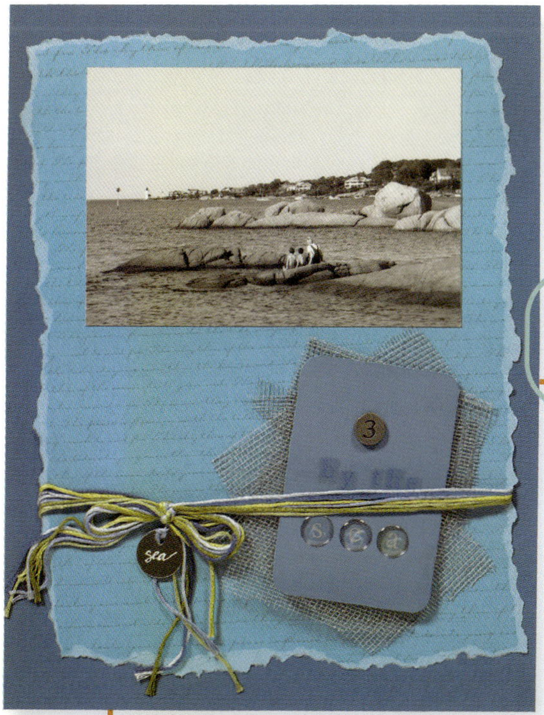

3 By the Sea

An excursion to the shore on a recent trip to Boston evoked many deep feelings in Marnie Flores. To capture her thoughts, she printed her recollections of the day in a script font on light blue card stock and tore the edges to give it the appearance of a page taken from a journal. To balance the black-and-white photo of her with her friend's sons, she made a tag for the title lettering from a paint swatch, placing scraps of window screening beneath it at the bottom of the page. Embroidery floss—chosen in the colors of the ocean—adds visual interest while providing a place to hang the engraved round metal tag.

Sources: Computer font is ICG Carpenter (used on background paper) downloaded off the Internet. Alphabet stickers by SEI. Eyelet number, alphabet pebbles, and metal tag by Making Memories. Engraver by Magic Scraps. Design by Marnie Flores.

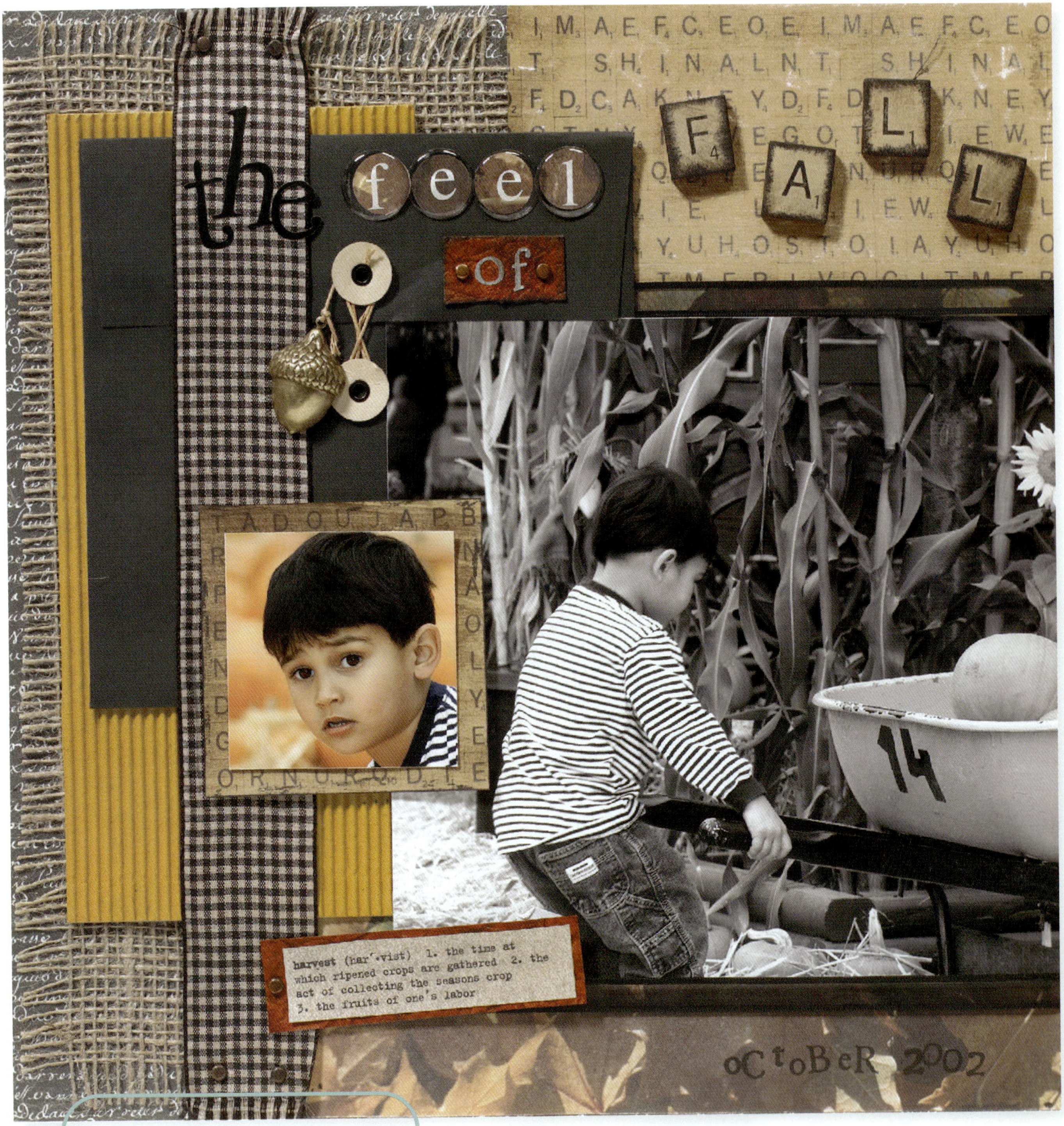

The Feel of Fall

Before Lilac Chang moved to sunny California, she had always lived in places where there was a noticible change of seasons. In her new home state with its fairly constant weather, she finds she misses the brilliant colors of autumn. Last fall, Lilac took her son to a pumpkin patch and enjoyed watching him play with the pumpkins, sunflowers, hay, and wheelbarrows. Wanting to celebrate the feeling of fall, she gathered her photos and set out to make this page. Lilac created her two-page photo collage with a variety

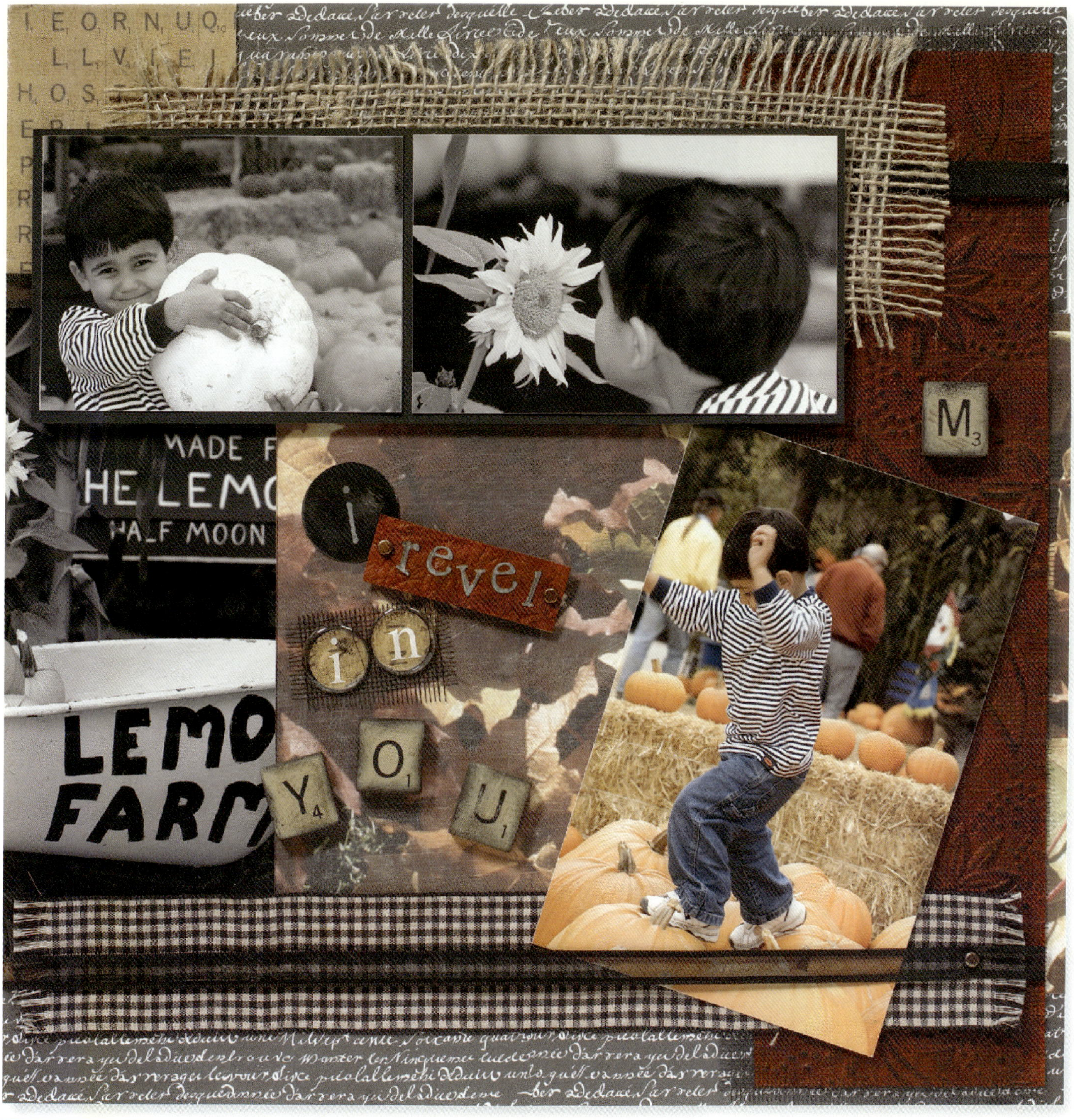

of textural materials, including sheer and checked ribbons, burlap, embossed papers, and assorted metal accents. She sanded wooden Scrabble tiles and inked them with a rich walnut color and then used the walnut ink to darken other elements on her page, unifying the design.

Sources: Patterned papers by 7Gypsies (scrabble and handwriting) and Print Blocks (leaves). Corrugated paper by All Night Media. Mesh paper by Magenta. Stickers by Sonnets for Creative Imaginations ("the," "of," and "revel"), Doodlebug Design ("I"), and Making Memories (definition). Rubber stamps by PSX. Page pebbles by Making Memories. Brads by Lost Treasures. Design by Lilac Chang.

Just the Beginning

Danelle Johnson hand-colored a close-up photo of autumn leaves to make the stunning background for this layout. She also color-washed the photos of her daughter and her daughter's playmate with brown to soften their images (see page 14 for more on hand tinting). Fibers, crumpled paper, and fabric in subdued tones add to the fall texture.

Sources: Patterned papers by Magenta. Letter stickers by Flavia for Colorbök. Fibers by Rubba Dub Dub. Button by JHB International. Design by Danelle Johnson.

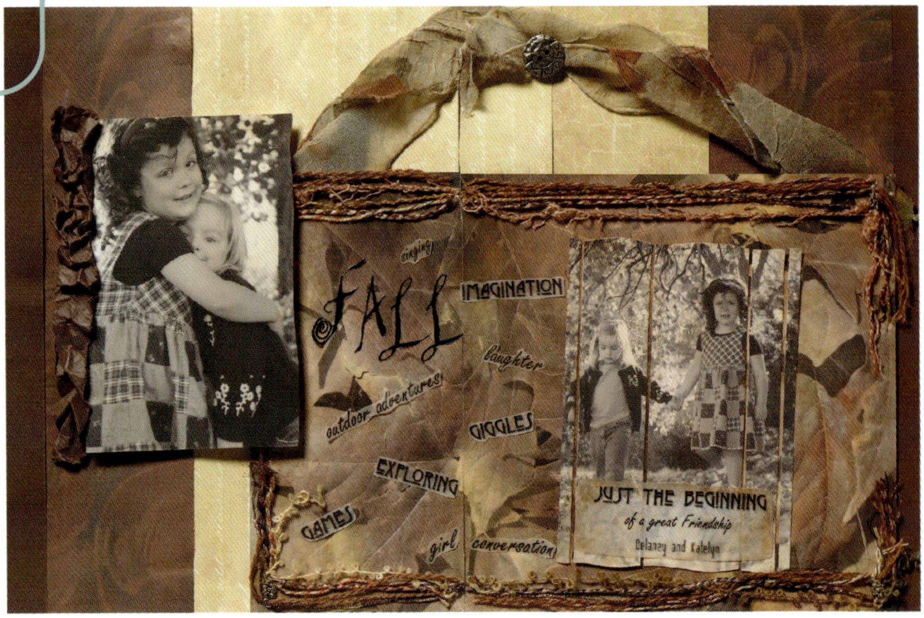

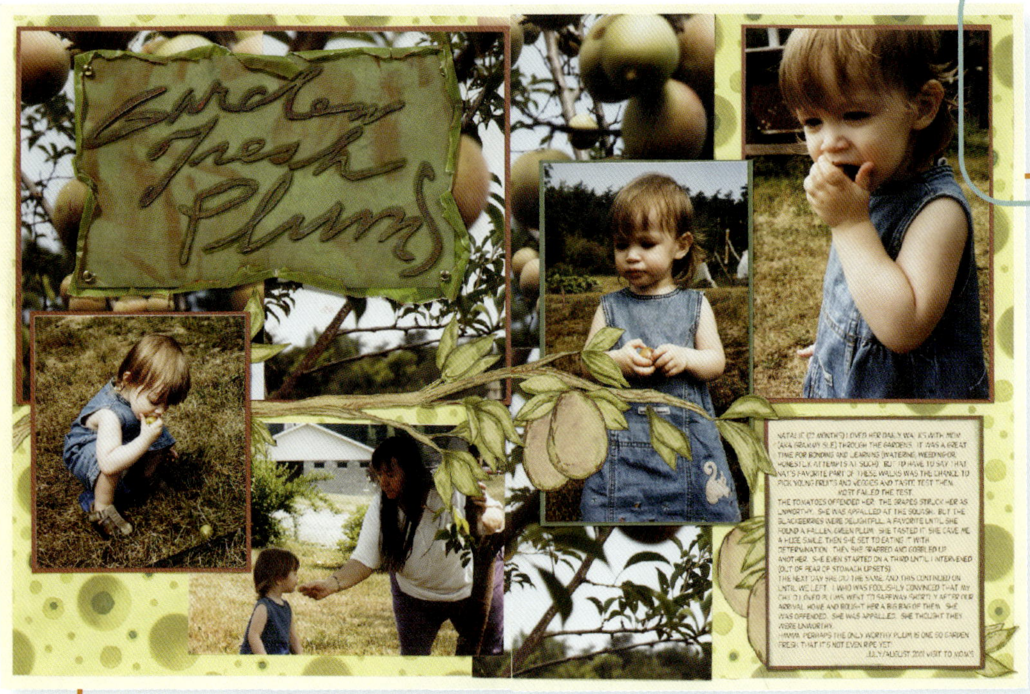

Garden-Fresh Plums

Even though the fruit hadn't reached its peak of ripeness, Nicole Gartland's daughter Natalie was delighted by the flavor of the fallen green plums in her grandmother's garden. Nicole snapped a number of great photos of Natalie enjoying the sweet fruit as well as some shots of the tree branches themselves, which serve as a backdrop for the page title and other photos. To re-create the branches of the plum tree, Nicole sketched her own version to span across the center of her layout. She shaded the plum branch with colored pencils and outlined the details with fine-tip pens. To make the title block, she cut the lettering from card stock, colored it with an ink pad, and glued it to green vellum. She then traced the letters on the back of the vellum with marker to create a shadowed effect. She layered a second, slightly larger piece of green vellum behind the title piece, rumpled the edges, and attached it with brads.

Sources: Patterned paper by Magenta. Vellum by Paper Adventures. Brads by Premiere Grip. The plum branch is Nicole's design (pattern on page 47). Design by Nicole Gartland.

patterns

Metamorphosis
page 43

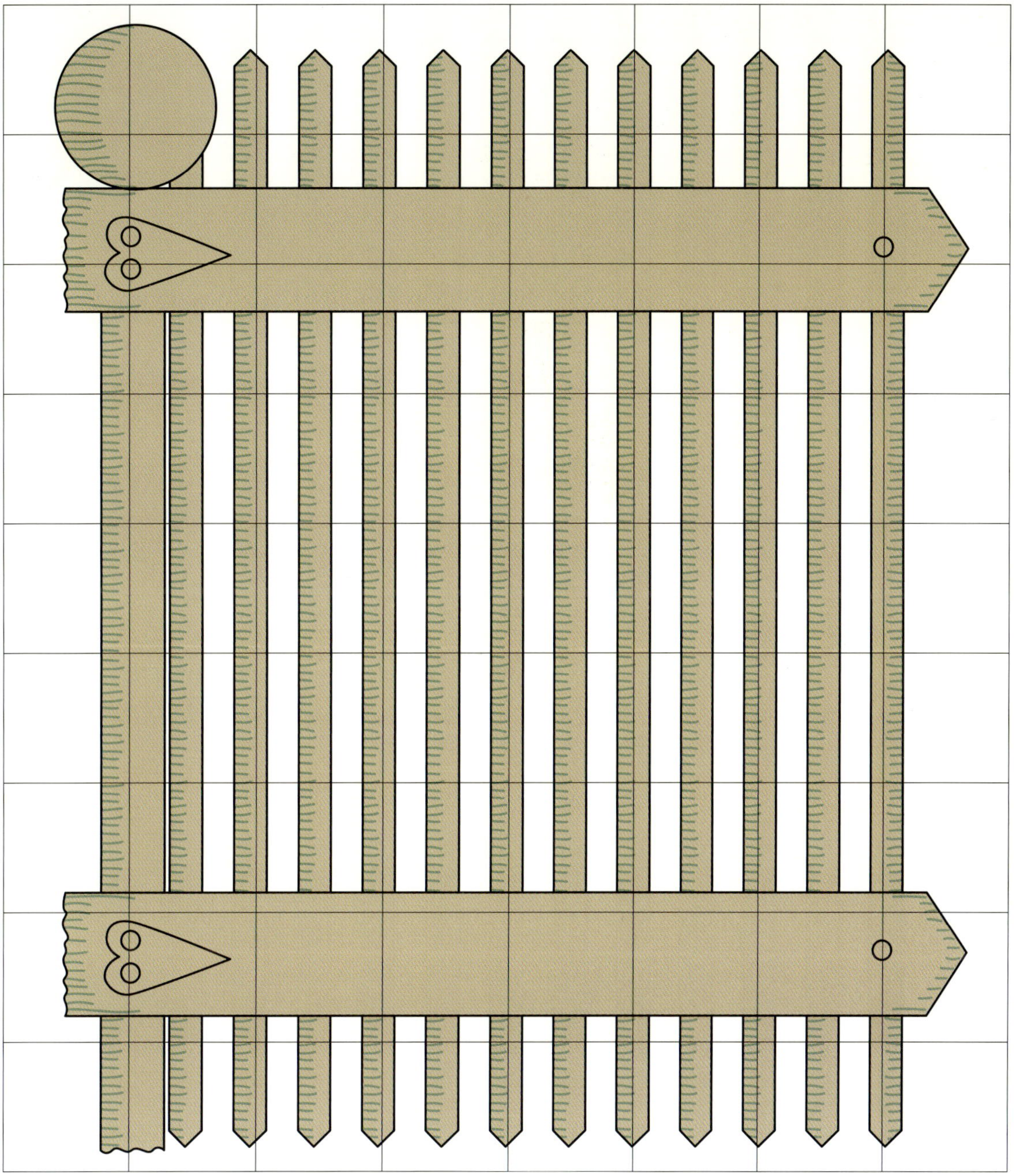

1 Square = 1 Inch

Garden-Fresh Plums
page 46

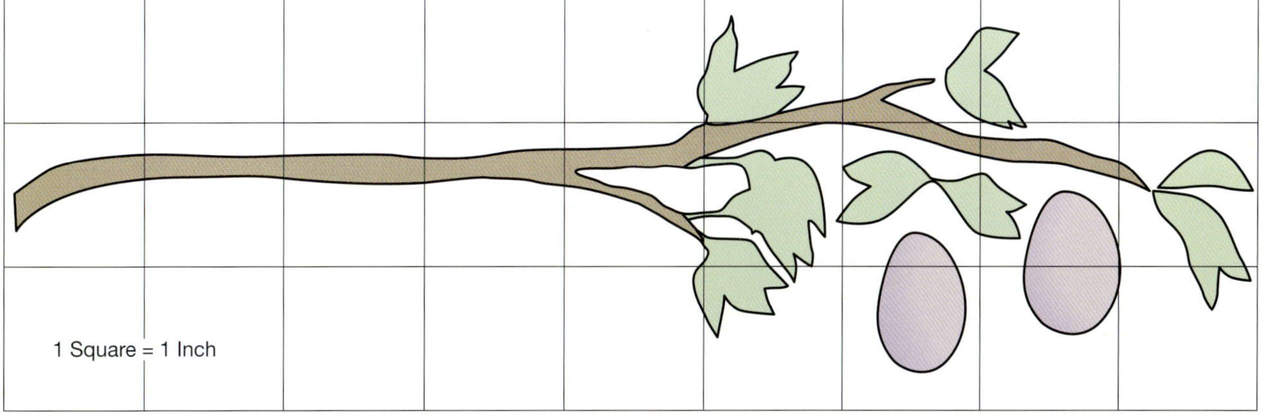

Better Homes and Gardens®
Creative Collection™

Director, Editorial Administration
Michael L. Maine

Editor-in-Chief
Beverly Rivers

Executive Editor Karman Wittry Hotchkiss

Editorial Manager
Ann Blevins

Art Director
Brenda Drake Lesch

Copy Chief Mary Heaton
Administrative Assistant Lori Eggers
Contributing Editor Laura Holtorf Collins
Contributing Graphic Designer Susie G. Rider
Contributing Copy Editor Kathy Roth Eastman

Vice President, Publishing Director
William R. Reed

Group Publisher Steve Levinson
Senior Marketing Manager Suzy Johnson

Meredith
CORPORATION

Chairman and CEO
William T. Kerr

In Memoriam
E. T. Meredith III (1933-2003)

Publishing Group President
Stephen M. Lacy
Magazine Group President
Jack Griffin
Publishing Group Executive Vice President
Jerry Kaplan

ISBN 1-60140-160-4